① "By failing to prepare, you're preparing to fail."

② Page 202.

# 44 Soccer Midfielder Mistakes to Avoid

Mirsad Hasic

# DEDICATION

I dedicate this book to my wife.

# CONTENTS

## ACKNOWLEDGMENTS

I would like to thank my family for their support.

# About Me and My Work

Hi, my name is Mirsad Hasic.

For those who may not be familiar with my work, allow me to explain a bit about my approach and style. The first thing I want to highlight is that I bring as much real-world information to the pages as I can.

Anyone can do a little research and write around a topic, but that's not my way. I like to get involved because you're involved, and so I need to know what it is that you'll be going through.

Everything you find in my books is researched thoroughly and experienced personally. I then pass on my findings and experiences, whenever appropriate, to you the reader. This is an approach to writing which helps me to connect better with my audience.

# I, We, and You...

You will notice throughout this book how I write in the first person "I" quite a lot. This is deliberate. It is to make your journey more interesting and the reading experience less pressuring. There are too many impersonal soccer related guides on sale today. Well, that's one approach I make sure to avoid. The "I" accounts in this book are more likely to get your focus too. These are what relate to some of the things I write about on a more personal level.

I also use "we" on occasions as well. This is because I have been where you are at now, to a greater or lesser extent, and know what you're going through. Therefore, we're in this together, and that helps you to pick up on similarities much easier.

And finally there is the "you" approach. I use the "you" in this book because I'm addressing you, my reader, directly.

# Introduction

This book is quite unlike most other midfielder books on the market today. To begin with, it's not a book full of boring, difficult-to-understand pages. There are already plenty of those out there, most of which don't teach players anything new. This book offers a fresh new approach.

I have written it in an easy-to-understand format that is both useful and entertaining. Anyone who is looking to develop and improve their game skills as a midfielder is in the right place. These pages inform you, the reader, and motivate you toward taking positive action.

This book covers not only the physical but also the mental side of being a great midfielder. In these chapters you will learn what all successful players do to reach greatness. By following their examples, you too will be able to take your game up to a whole new level.

# Why Most Soccer Players Fail

There are many midfielders around today who are fast, strong and talented. They also have the physical features a player needs to become successful. Yet despite all this, so many of them never make the grade, not even close. Why is that? The answer is a simple one.

They lack the proper knowledge and don't have the right mindset to take them where they need to go. The good news for you is that these are not the kind of things you will have to worry about, not now that you have this book. You are going to learn three fundamental principles.

The first is what you need to do. The second is what not to do. And the third fundamental is how to develop the right mindset to make great things happen. Not only is your game going to improve, but all areas of your life will change for the better too. That is, providing you take action on your newfound knowledge of course.

# What This Book Will Show You

This book will show you the 44 things that all great midfielders did, and still do, to become successful. From Patrick Vieira to Steven Gerard, this book covers them all. By understanding the 44 mistakes to avoid, you develop 44 new ways to do things, the right way. That is why this book is so empowering.

# How to Approach This Book?

Prepare to discover the unknown. In this book you will realize the common mistakes that amateur midfielders make. If they go unnoticed, these things can mean the difference between success and failure.

These mistakes can, and often do, have a huge negative impact on the way a midfielder performs. Read this book from cover to cover. You can then identify and deal with any errors that apply to you and your game.

This book will also make you aware of the problems associated with your belief system. These are the little messages which govern your thoughts, words, and actions, or inactions, as the case may be.

Midfielders who perform below par often fall short not because they lack the physical talent. They fall short, more often than not, because they don't believe in themselves 100 percent.

The primary purpose of this book is to open your mind to the things you haven't been aware of until now. You will discover new ideas, the best practices, and get to develop a sharper awareness for the midfielder position. You are going to learn how to identify errors in your game as you develop your playing style.

Just as important is that you will discover what to watch out for. This ensures you don't fall prey to the often latent traps during a game. These are the things in soccer that can hurt and hinder your attempts to perform well on the field.

OK, so without further ado let's get started. Positive change is coming your way and it begins right now. Here's is a quick rundown so that you can see what to expect as you read through these exciting chapters

- **Strength and Stamina**: Find out what you need to do to reach peak physical fitness so that you can last longer on the field.
- **Mastering Tackles**: Learn how to master the art of recovering the ball from your opponent, without getting booked.
- **Bend it like Beckham**: How to master the art of sending lethal crosses that result in goals for your team.
- **Avoiding Yellow Cards**: Learn how to avoid getting dragged into receiving yellow cards.
- **How to Compensate for Shortcomings**: How to compensate for any lack in strength required for your role on the field. Find out how to use your own skills to fill the void.

- **Dealing with Counter Attacks**: How to master counter attacks both in a defensive and offensive capacity. Learn how to do this regardless of the role you take on the field.
- **Speed**: Discover how the fastest wingers in the world outrun their opponents, and what you should do to mimic them.
- **The Last 20 Minutes**: How to react to different game changes at the most critical moments of the competition.
- **Working the Referee**: Find out how to make sure the ref stays fair throughout the entire game, and the ways can influence his decisions.
- **Making the Right Decisions**: How to perfect your decision-making process by learning from the mistakes you make.
- **Super Mascherano**: Find out the one thing that all the great defensive midfielders in the world focus on to become the best.
- **The Complete Midfielder**: Find out how to take on different roles and play in different positions. See how you too can become an indispensable player in your team.
- **The Right Way to Tackle**: The four simple considerations that will see you win 90 percent of the tackles you make throughout a game.
- **Giving Directions**: Know how to instruct your teammates in set pieces and corner kicks.
- **Why Mind Games Matter**: Find out how to take on different roles and play in different positions. See how you too can become an indispensable player in your team.

- **Managing Anger**: How best to control your temper to prevent you from flipping-out and upsetting the game.
- **Intimidation Tactics**: Learn how to become more feared and intimidating to your opponents. See how you can create an effect on your opponents that makes them soft around you.
- **Using Both Feet**: Find out why playing with both legs is such an important skill. Learn how to train yourself so that you can play with both feet equally.
- **Correct Positioning**: Discover how to position yourself so that you can reach and clear more balls without using too many tackles.
- **Passing and Shooting Skills**: Find new ways to enhance your passing and shooting skills so you can add extra attacking solutions for your team.
- **Lead the Way with Good Communication**: Find out how to lead on the soccer field. Know the best ways to communicate with your teammates in different situations throughout the game.
- **The Winning Formula**: Learn of the one thought and act that will take your success to stratospheric levels when followed correctly.
- **Avoid Dangerous Mistakes**: Know how to avoid the type of mistakes that can break a midfielder's career in an instant.

- **Maintain Motivation**: Get to stay motivated and power-hungry at all times. Learn the secret behind why so many great players last longer than their peers.
- **Know Your Opponents**: Know what to study about your opponents. Find out how to uncover their tricks, strengths and weak points during a game.
- **Different Weather Conditions**: Learn how to adjust when playing in different weather conditions. Here we look at wet, windy, and overly bright days.
- **The Comeback**: What to do when your team is behind in the score. Know how to prevent the rival team exploiting the soccer rules which allow them to control the tempo of the game by wasting time.
- **Avoid Provocation**: Know what to do when an opponent tries to mess with your game using unfair actions or words. Learn how not to lose your focus in these situations, and get him punished for his unfair play.
- **The Confidence Boost**: Here we look at the scientific way to build self-confidence.
- **Avoid Injury**: Find out what exercises you need to perform to avoid becoming injury prone.
- **Game Preparation**: Learn how to use your mental powers the night before a competition so that you can perform at your very best on game day.

- **The Way to Manage Fear**: Find out how to become fearless on the field and how to remove your own fears of getting hurt or injured.
- **Warm-up like a Pro**: Know how to warm up properly before the competition starts so you can use all your physical capabilities the second the game begins.
- **Make the Most of Mistakes**: See how you can make every mistake you make count for something. Discover how you can make your performance 10 times better in just six months.

You have all of this and more besides…

# 1. Not Understanding the Roles of Different Midfielders

Determining the different types of midfielder is something that's important. It helps you to understand the requirements and demands of whichever role you take on.

Below are the main roles/distributions of soccer midfield players, starting with the Central Midfielder.

# Central Midfielder (CM)

Central midfielders provide a crucial link between defense and attack. These are the guys who may fulfill many duties during a single game. For the most part, their job is to operate in the middle third of the field. You will often hear people call a central midfielder a Regista or playmaker.

He can act as the director of the entire team. A Regista is the second coach of the side, only he's active on the field.

He is the one who decides how most of the team's attacks will go. The Regista of any team will be the midfielder on the side. He is able to play both offensive and defensive roles to great effect.

The Regista will lie back in front of his defensive line, closer to his penalty area. From here he is able to provide extra protection. He will help cut the ball anywhere between the two penalty areas. For this reason, some analysts refer to him as the box-to-box Midfielder.

He will cut the ball at the back and support his teammates in the front. He gets to control the tempo of the game and distribute balls to anywhere on the field. He does all these things and more according to what he can see and how he reads the game.

In general, a Regista will have strong leadership skills. He plays with determination and controlled aggression when he attempts to win the ball. He has great stamina and a high level of physical fitness.

Registas are the players who run the most during a game. Besides all these things, they have excellent passing and shooting skills too.

Two of the best Registas of the last decade are Liverpool's captain Steven Gerard, and the Italian legend Andrea Pirlo.

# Defensive Midfielder (DM)

A defensive midfielder, or holding midfielder, is a soccer position which adds an extra layer of defense. This is the player who holds to his position in the center of his team, or behind it when his side is attacking.

This includes when his defenders move to the front to help in corners and set pieces. He should always stay close to his team's defense. If ever he gets dragged away from his position, he opens up a channel of attack that the opposition can exploit.

The position depends on his ability to position himself in the right place at the right moment. When positioned well, he is able to intercept the ball or stay close to it.

He is in a good position anytime the other team tries to make a counter attack. His job is to either defuse the attack or hold it back until his teammates return to their defensive positions.

The role of a DM demands excellent tackling skills. He also needs to be good at getting rid of the ball. This is his number one priority.

In general, the DM makes short and quite simple passes to his more attacking teammates. In certain situations though, he may get involved in more difficult passes. It all depends on the team's strategy at the time.

There are two great defensive midfielders to learn from. Once is the France and Arsenal legendary captain, Patrick Vieira. The other is Barcelona's number one DM, Sergio Busquets.

## Attacking Midfielder (AM)

An attacking midfielder is the one responsible for moving the ball from the midfield toward the front line of his team, or to the two attackers direct. He is located in the advanced midfield position. That's somewhere between the central midfield and the team's forwards.

For this role, you should have excellent vision, good timing, and outstanding passing skills. Passing is important for this position.

By that, I mean you have to be and willing to pass the ball to a player in a better scoring position than yourself. This is not position for ball-hoggers, or someone who has a strong desire to score lots of goals for their own glory.

You can split the role of the attacking midfielder into two types. One is the traditional playmaker, and the other a striker. Which role is right for you will depend on a few things, those being your capabilities, your preferences and your goal scoring ability.

Two great examples of traditional playmakers are France's legend Zinedine Zidane, and Mesut Ozil. In fact, Ozil is one of the best playmakers in the world, and has been for the last 10 years. He has an excellent rate for creating chances in both the Spanish league and the English premier league.

For the second striker we have the best player of the twentieth century to look up to. In case you haven't guessed, I'm talking about the Argentine legend, Diego Armando Maradona.

## Wingers (RW & LW)

In modern day soccer, the term winger (also called a wide player) refers to a non-defender position. A winger is basically a midfielder who plays wide on one of the two flanks.

As for the role, the winger has a couple of main responsibilities. He supports his full back, the right or the left back, as well as taking the ball from the middle to the front.

The winger's role demands that you have excellent crossing skills. You must also have a strong foot, one that you have programmed to shoot powerful, accurate shots on demand. And of course, all wingers should be fast, and the faster the better.

In fact, 90 percent of the fastest players in the world right now are wingers. This includes the likes of Alexis Sanchez, Arjen Robben, Eden Hazard and Gareth Bale.

# 2. Not Being Able to Defend in Corner Kicks and Set Pieces

Part of the role of any box-to-box, or holding midfielder, is to be able to partake in corner kicks and set pieces. This is in both an offensive and defensive capacity. Most players who take these roles on are strong and can perform powerful shots.

Their strength lets them either score from a header or clear a corner away from their penalty area. The Belgian, Marouane Fellaini, and Ivorian, Yaya Toure, are two good examples that fit the bill here.

This rule doesn't apply to short midfielders though. It's even less important for playmakers whose job in corner kicks and set pieces is to stand on the goal line. That's if the player is a defensive midfielder of course. Arsenal's Francis Coquelin is one example. He's just 1.78m.

There are those too who stand in front of the penalty area to collect the ball and start a new attack. Or if not a new attack, they will at least try to prevent any opponents from kicking the ball outside the penalty area.

# How to Improve Your Explosive Jump

There are five basic things you need to be good at if you're to master headers. The first thing you need, and this is important, is to have a good explosive jump. The second crucial trait is intuition.

Your ability to know where the ball is likely to end up is something that will make or break your header attempt. The third thing is to work out real quick the positions of all rival attackers who are likely to go for the ball. That includes those behind you as well as the ones in front.

The fourth thing is confidence. In other words, you have to be confident that you can reach the ball before anyone else. You also have to be confident that you can perform a successful header. The fifth and final attribute is your ability to send the ball to a safe place, and that means well away from danger.

# The Importance of the Explosive Jump

I will use the Portuguese superstar, Cristiano Ronaldo, to illustrate the explosive jump. If you haven't seen him performing headers yet, then I urge you to find some clips of his jumping style online. You can learn a lot from the way Ronaldo jumps and heads the ball.

Ronaldo's fans call him the Complete Ron because he is the ultimate complete player. When it comes to headers, he's currently one of the best jumpers in European soccer. This is even more impressive when you consider his height.

At just 1.85 m, Ronaldo is not that tall. Yet besides this disadvantage, his jumping style is better than his taller peers. That includes players on both the attacking and the defensive lines.

Being able to jump higher than any taller player marking him is impressive, but it's not the only thing that is. Ronaldo's ability to head the ball with power and accuracy is what makes his headers so special.

For me, the most impressive thing of all is that he doesn't need a lot of space to prepare for his jumps. When you consider the height, power, and the accuracy he reaches, this is a rare talent.

So Ronaldo is not only good at headers, he's exceptional. Perhaps the most impressive thing about his header skills is that he wasn't like this early on in his career. This is something he has developed from the ground up.

I can cast my mind back to when Ronaldo played for Sporting Lisbon. I can remember him at Manchester United too, in the premier league. Don't get me wrong, he was still good back then. But he wasn't the great jumper that he is today.

Those years he spent at Manchester United were the years where he got to develop his game. He left Man U with 118 goals in 292 games.

That's not bad, but it's nothing compared to how he exploded at Madrid. We're now talking 321 goals in 307 games, at the last count.

The point I want to now make is how Ronaldo's impressive header skills came about. It's important to note that this is not a natural talent.

His ability came about as a direct result of relentless hard work. He knew what he needed to do and he went on a mission to achieve it.

In fact, Ronaldo became obsessed about enhancing his performance in this area. He decided to take things to a whole new level. He got a famous athlete involved, Usain Bolt, who is the fastest man on planet.

He asked Bolt to teach him how to run faster, so he did. He also took lessons from professional NBA players.

He asked them to teach him how to improve his jump, so they did. They showed him how to extend his body to the max so that he could make explosive take-offs.

With their help, Ronaldo didn't just get good, he got real good. At the end of his training mission, Ronaldo was able to jump higher than almost anyone who marked him.

Today, at the time of writing this book, Ronaldo is one of the best attacking players in the history of soccer. He has three Ballon D`ors and 17 million EUR as an annual salary.

That's a pretty hefty pay packet for a 30 year old. For anyone who's not familiar, The Ballon D`ors is an annual association football award by FIFA. It goes to the male player who performed the best soccer in the previous calendar year.

OK, so what can we take from Ronaldo's efforts? Well, to begin with, it just shows you how dedication and total commitment can make you great. Not all players are born with natural talents.

But then again, talent alone is not much use anyway, not without commitment and hard work. Many players get to be great not because they have natural talent. They become great because they never ever give up on themselves, no matter what or who stands in their way.

If you want to become a great midfielder, you must adopt the same attitude. And with regards to performing great headers, know that it all starts with the explosive jump.

Explosive jumps, also called power jumps, will work miracles for you. Don't ever underestimate the power of headers.

I have seen both defenders and attackers score some great goals from these. And for the record, these guys are not always tall either.

So whatever you do, if you're a little on the short side, don't let that put you off working on your explosive jumps. In fact, it's even more important to work at them if you're a bit shorter than most other players.

## How to Improve Your Jump

If you want to improve your explosive jumps you're going to need some gym time.

This is because you have to exercise the muscles responsible for the jumping process. These are your abs and leg muscles, including the calves.

Make a note of all the exercises below and fit them into your workout routine.

These are the exercises that will develop all the right muscles. Once you develop these muscles, you will achieve stronger, higher jumps on the field.

## Your Jump Exercises

-   Abs crunches: 4–6 sets, for 15-20 repetitions.
-   Spiderman Plank Crunch: 4–6 reps, 10 reps for each side.
-   Planks: 3-4 sets, 1–2 minutes each.
-   Jump Squat: 4-6 sets, 10–12 reps each and one minute's rest between each set.
-   Frog Jumps: 4-6 sets, 10–12 reps each and one minute's rest between each set.
-   Squats: High rep range, low to moderate weights.
-   Calves: Do calf raises (seated and raised) as well as leg presses on the smith machine.

OK, so these are the exercises you must do. They are the ones that will help to improve your vertical jump, enabling you to reach new heights.

Having a good jump is only part of the deal though. A jump will get you to where you want to be, but you still you need to know how to perform great headers once you're up there.

# Judging Where the Ball Will End Up

Predicting where the ball is most likely to end up after a play requires experience, and plenty of it. This is only something you can get by playing a lot of soccer and by studying other games. Judging where the ball is going to end up is not something you can get by reading a book.

A book can help you, as it can show you how to gain the experience you need. But it's then up to you to take the action necessary to develop this important skill.

Remember, experience does not only come from physical practice but by observing as well. Your ability to read the game is something that will make or break a situation. It all depends on how well or how poor you do it.

Once you have figured out where the ball is most likely to go, you have to then start running in that direction. You do this hoping that no one else has yet figured out where the ball will end up.

Being fast is important, of course, but even more important here is your ability to read the game well. It helps too, when you are familiar with your opponent's style of play.

# Consider the Positions of the Attackers

Never overlook the positions of the attackers around you. This is crucial to the outcome of your efforts.

Always be mindful of the fact that an attacker will often sneak up from behind. When he's successful, he gets to hit the ball toward the near post before anyone spots him.

Don't let this happen to you. To prevent it, you have to determine the positions of your opponents relative to where the ball will end up. This way you are much better informed before you decide on your next moves.

Maybe you will go for the ball direct, or perhaps you will prepare to block it after the opponent kicks it. Whatever you decide, the more you know about your surroundings the better the outcome will be.

# Using Your Body to Restrict the Movements of an Opponent

From the moment the referee starts counting for a corner it will be all out war. There is a real scrum as players fight for the best position inside the penalty area. This is a time that calls for you to use all your physical strength.

You need strength so that you can block the movements of the opponent you're marking. You aim is simple. You want to prevent him from being able to take the best position to jump or move toward the ball as it arrives in the area.

# How to Block Your Opponent

Whenever possible, the best way to block your opponent is by using your chest and hands. You have to be mindful of a couple of things here though.

The first is to make sure the referee doesn't see you getting too physical with your opponent. The second is to make sure you're not too aggressive in your approach.

Too much jostling and you could end up in a fight (you how it can be). But you could also make a foul during the corner kick. If that happens, there will be a penalty awarded to the rival side.

Send the Ball to the Safest Possible Place

If you play a header from a corner kick or a foul, there is something you must NEVER do. That is, you must never send the ball toward any opponent who faces the penalty area or is standing on its edge.

If you do send the ball their way, then beware. The opponent is now in a good position to start a fresh attack. He will most likely get to start his attack before your teammates have had time to reorganize.

What you need to do is send your headers to the sides of the penalty area. Whenever you can, play them high. This way you get to force the ball to take longer before it reaches the ground.

What this does is give you and your teammate's a couple of extra seconds to prepare. It doesn't sound like much, I know, but it is. A couple of extra seconds gives you enough time to reorganize yourselves before the next attack.

The final thing I need to mention here is to also avoid sending headers toward the center of the penalty area. This is because there will often be a player from the rival side hanging around there.

He will usually be a stopper or a short striker. These guys are opportunistic, hoping for a chance to receive the ball. If they do, then that's bad news for you as they get to smash it right toward the net.

So your job is to make things harder for them, and you do this by sending your headers toward the left or right edges.

# 3. You Get Sent off with Cards When Playing as a DM or CM

Whenever you can, always save your first yellow card toward the end of the game. As a central midfielder your role forces you to make a lot of tackles.

Any yellow card you get in the first 40 or 50 minutes of the game will affect your performance. The reason for this is because you become more cautious. That means you won't go after the ball with your full capacity and strength for fear of getting a second card.

As you can see, getting an early yellow card puts you at a huge disadvantage. Your opponents will be quite happy about it though. An early yellow card for you gives them more opportunity to keep all their balls.

Why? Because they know you will do anything to avoid a second yellow card, and so they exploit that fact. They now concentrate a decent amount of their attacks on your side of the defense. This means the opponents have a better chance to reach your goal area.

They understand it's unlikely that you will make aggressive tackles against them. If you do end up with a second yellow card, your opponents then get to outnumber your team by one player. That then creates even more danger for your side. This is why it's so important to avoid an early yellow card, and especially a second yellow card.

Let's look at two "card prone" defensive midfielders, Felipe Melo and Mathieu Flamini. They have both lost their edge on the field, as well as the positions in their teams. This is because of the number of yellow and red cards they have received.

I have never seen any of them complete 10 consecutive games without getting suspended. You almost expect these guys to get a direct red card or exceed the number or yellow cards allowed for a player to have in each league.

There is only one way for you to steer clear of this problem. That is, you will have to avoid any unwanted tackles or fouls, especially at the beginning of the game. This includes:

# Aggressive Tackles in "Safe" Areas

One example of tackling in a safe area is to tackle an opponent in his own half. Another is to tackle your opponent on either side of the center line. Also avoid aggressive tackles on your opponents whenever there are two or more players covering you.

## Tackling from Behind

Another thing you should never do is to tackle a player from behind. There may be the odd situation where it's necessary, but in general, avoid this kind of tackle at all costs. If anyone tricks you into making a tackle from behind, the referee will more than likely send you off with a red card.

The soccer rule is strict and clear about tackles from the rear. Because this type of tackle requires an automatic red card, many refs will send a player off without giving it a second thought. He will do this even if you managed to touch the ball, which is the only reason that cancels the foul.

# Taking off Your T-shirt After Scoring a Goal

Despite being wrong, this is something that still happens quite a bit. I'm not sure why because players know it's a punishable offense. Maybe it's the excitement that sweeps over them the moment they score a goal.

There are some guys who just can't resist celebrating a goal by taking off their shirt. They usually wave it around in the air like a triumphant flag. What follows next is the inevitable yellow card for misbehavior.

Now, just imagine making a foul once the game is back in full swing. Ouch! It means that the player who was so happy and excited just a short while ago now receives his second yellow card. The referee then has no choice but to send him off the field.

 One mistake made by some players is that they forget they have a yellow card from much earlier in the game. So when they rip off their shirt in celebration of a goal, their daft act has just got them sent off.

You can imagine the look on their faces when it suddenly dawns on them what has happened. All the begging in the world won't usually sway the ref's decision either.

# Wasting Time When Playing a Throw-in or an Indirect Free Kick

This is something that most referees have zero tolerance with. Time wasting gives an unfair advantage to the side wasting the time, but that's not all it does. It also takes the entertainment factor out of a game, and that's not what fans have paid to see.

So a referee will be sensitive to any attempt of any player who wastes time toward the end of a game. If he suspects it's going on, he will issue an immediate yellow card. Knowing this doesn't stop a lot of players from trying though.

They try to disguise their time wasting antics, and sometimes they're successful. But too much too often, and it soon becomes clear what's going on. If you want to waste a little time, be mindful of what you're doing and try to think how the ref might be viewing things.

You should never try to waste time if you already have a yellow card, especially if you play as a DM. I would say only time-waste if you play on the attacking line, as an AM or a winger.

If you do play on the attacking line as an AM or a winger, you must never time-waste if you already have a yellow card. It's just not worth the gamble.

Tip: Leave wasting time to the team attackers and wingers. These are the guys who are least likely to take yellow cards.

# Touching the Ball with Your Hands in a Safe Place

I'm going to cast your mind back to the 2006 World Cup in Germany. There was one game in particular that fans will never forget.

The only problem is that it's remembered for all the wrong reasons. This game was between Portugal and The Netherlands, in the quarter final. It is so infamous that it even has its own special name.

They call it "The Battle of Nuremberg." It was a battle too. The Russian referee, Valentin Ivanov, gave out a total of 20 cards in that competition. There were 16 yellow and four reds handed out to 12 different players of both sides. This was not what you might call a well behaved game where sportsmanship prevailed.

One of those four red cards went to Portugal's player, Costinha. He actually received two consecutive yellow cards. The first incident was an early, unwanted tackle at the thirtieth minute.

The second was in the last minute of the first half. It was after he tried to touch the ball with his hand in the center of the field. The ref saw that, and off Costinha went.

No handballs in safe areas.

# Acting / Simulation

If you pretend or simulate that an opponent has hit you, and the referee catches it, you're in big trouble. He will hand you a yellow card without any hesitation at all. This kind of sneaky tactic is quite common in modern soccer.

Players do this as a way to convince the referee of the wrongdoing, which never actually happened. The hope is that the ref will send the player off or at least give him a yellow card.

The only way you can do this and get away with it, is if the referee is too far away to see what's really going on.

But if he's close enough to catch the sneaky simulation, then it will backfire on you. It will be you who receives a yellow card, not the other player. Such humiliation will more than likely have a negative effect on the way you play the rest of the game too.

## When You're Simulated On

Netherland's defender, Khaled Boulahrouz, received his second yellow card after he was simulated on by Portugal's player, Luis Figo. This was during the battle of Nuremberg just mentioned. It happened when Figo was running behind Boulahrouz, whose hand accidentally touched the Portuguese's face.

Figo then threw himself to the ground, making it look as though he had been deliberately whacked. He hadn't been whacked; he was just taking advantage of the situation. It worked too, and the referee sent the Dutch player off the field with a second yellow card.

## Grabbing an Attacker's T-Shirt from Behind

Grabbing a player's t-shirt from the back is a surefire way to get you an unwanted yellow card.

If the play is a long way from your goal area, you're even more likely to get a yellow card.

This is because the player's whose shirt you grab poses no immediate threat to you or your team. In other words, you did not do it in some desperate attempt to stop the opponent from scoring.

There are occasions when you have to stop an attacker using whatever means are available to you at the time. No one should condone such misconduct, but a little misbehavior is sometimes necessary.

Everyone does it from time to time, to some extent at least. This is especially the case if there is a real threat of the opponent scoring a goal unless you act fast. For example, when there is a counter attack going on and the opponents in the area outnumber you.

Still, this kind of behavior should always be the exception though, and never the norm. In other words, if you do feel the need to grab an attacker's shirt, try to be sensible about it. Only do it in situations that call for very desperate measures, and when the ref is not likely to see you.

There will be occasions on the field when a defensive midfielder is nutmegged or outrun. Perhaps he feels humiliated by the skilled, faster attacker. It can be tempting to lose one's cool in these situations. In fact, we see it happening all the time.

The defender grabs the attacker's t-shirt out of anger and frustration. Most moments of madness happen when the pressure is on. Even so, it's better to try and remain composed if you can.

Spontaneous outbursts like these rarely help a situation. Still, the nature of the game means there are never any guarantees how someone might act in the heat of the moment. We sometimes surprise ourselves by our spontaneous actions too.

But it's still important that you never forget that playing as a Regista or a DM makes you card-prone. This is why you in particular have to learn how to control your emotions when things get tough and rough on the field.

You need to look for the balance where you can stop an attack with proportional force. The idea is to be borderline tough. All that means is that you get to go in hard but with a minimal risk of getting a card.

Defensive midfielders will always be card-prone, that will never change. Your only real defense is to play smart and know your options at any given time. This is something that can only come about by knowing the danger, and with experience.

# 4. Not Able to Overcome a Lack in Physical Strength

All positions in soccer demand that the players have good physical strength. For some positions, it is better that the player is both tall and strong. For example, the team's goalkeepers or the two players in the center back.

Wherever you play on the field, you must have the physical attributes required for that role. If you fall short in any area, you need to have extra skills to make up for any loss. This is the only way to balance things out and compensate for any lack in physical strength.

As a midfielder, you don't have to be as concerned about your height as the goalkeeper. However, strength is not something you will want to fall short on in this position.

That's unless you can make up for the loss with some other skill(s) that will set you apart from your peers. Below are two examples of players who managed to do just that. Both of these guys lacked proper physical strength.

Let's now look at each of them in turn.

## Pep Guardiola

I'm sure you are familiar with Pep Guardiola, if not a big fan of the man. Guardiola is one of the best, if not the best, coaches in the world right now. He has this unique philosophical approach toward soccer. It shows too, through the team he coaches, Bayern Munich.

Back in time, his attacking style made him one of the best defensive midfielders of the 1990s. He was also Barcelona's captain for six consecutive years.

But here's a fact about Guardiola. He wasn't the guy that most coaches would have chosen to be their first defensive midfielder. That was before he found out how to fix things. Let me explain:

In his book, entitled "Herr Pep," Guardiola talks about his role on the field. He explains how he developed his game and became one of the best defensive midfielders in soccer.

He achieved all his ambitions despite his setbacks. For example, he lacked in speed and in goal scoring skills. He didn't even have a strong body, which is something most would say is crucial for the DM position.

So how did he do it, how could he succeed with so many shortcomings? Guardiola's answer was simple. He said that he realized early on that he would never be able to compete with many other players from a strength perspective.

Because of this, he knew he had to adapt if he was to excel in the game. So he decided to work on developing a skill he did feel qualified to pursue.

Guardiola's put all his time, energy, and focus into reading the game. This is something he became quite good at. So it made perfect sense to him, to then continue developing this ability still further.

His new focus was to take his skill from being quite good to exceptional. For him to get to the next level he studied countless hours of video.

He would study other player's games and their playing styles. He took endless notes, and then tested and retested himself constantly. He never gave up and he never stopped trying to improve.

Guardiola's commitment was relentless. His goal was simple, and that was to become a serious and highly competitive player.

He became so good at reading the game that he would often predict something happening long before it did.

That's "long before" in the soccer sense of course, not in actual time. This is a man who lasted for 11 years at Barcelona. He then went on to become the manager of one of the best teams in the history of soccer, Bayern Munich.

His starting point was to first realize what he was good at. In his case, it was reading the game. Guardiola then ran with that skill until he became brilliant at it. This simple approach was the secret behind his enormous success. This should be your approach too.

If you are to excel as a player and stand out from the pack, you have to zoom in on what you're good at and develop it as far as you can take it. We're all good at something, but we don't always know what that is. This is why you have to look deep inside your game until you find what your real strengths are.

They might not always be what you thought they were either. It might be your speed, passing skills, dribbling, or perhaps it's your shooting style. Whatever it is, you will know, or you will get to know, when you start looking into your strong points in great detail.

Get others involved too, if you need to. Sometimes, other people can see in us what we fail to see in ourselves. Once you know what you have to work on, stick with it until you become unbeatable.

Being good in a certain area, and then developing that skill(s) above all others, is a very smart move. It is something that will help to advance your career like no other.

And remember, it's important that you aim to become the best in that skill. Soccer clubs don't care too much about second best, not when it comes to choosing new players.

# Jesús Navas

The second player on this list is Jesús Navas. He is the Spanish winger who currently plays for the English club, Manchester City. Navas has won the World Cup and the European Championship with his country Spain.

He has also won two UEFA Cups with Sevillia and one Premier league title with Man City. So you know that we're looking at a world class winger here. But like Pep Guardiola above, Jesus Navas also had his setbacks.

At just 1.72 m, he is one of the shortest players in both English and European soccer. Navas weighs in at only 150 lbs (about 68kg). You might be wondering how, given his stature and weight, he ever made it, especially as a winger.

Even more impressive is that got into two of the most physically challenging leagues in the world of soccer. This is a position that even the biggest, tallest, wingers find tough. So how did he do it, how did he manage to compensate for the areas he lacked in?

If you don't already know, or haven't yet guessed it, he got to where he is because of his speed. And because of this, he has become one of the fastest wingers in the whole world. Speed like his is incredibly useful for this position.

It's not only the ability to run fast that makes Navas so valuable. It's also because he can change his direction real quick while dribbling. Watch him play or make a run on the wing and you will see him fly like a human bullet.

So Navas realized he could still make the grade with his lightweight, shorter body. Like Pep Guardiola, he zoomed in and worked on what he was good, and without worrying too much about the areas he fell short in.

So in this case his biggest asset was his speed, ability to dodge, and crosses. He kept working at these things until he became the player he is today. As you can see, there can still be hope in what most others would see as hopeless situations.

By the way, I have covered everything you need to know about pace and speed in a late chapter.

# 5. Not Being Good at Tackling

If you want to learn everything about tackling, then I recommend you study the skills of some of the greats. I will suggest four defensive midfielders in particular. The first two are legendary stoppers who have since retired from competitive soccer. The last two are still playing and considered by many as the best tacklers in the world at this moment in time. Let's take a closer look at these guys.

# The World's Best Tacklers

- Claude Makélélé
- Patrick Vieira
- Nemanja Matić
- Francis Coquelin

The first two, Makélélé and Vieira, helped to form the best national team France has ever seen. Both of them assisted France to reach two World Cup finals, one of which they won. They also helped France win the 2000 Euro tournament.

Let's look at their profiles in a little more detail, to see what makes them so special.

## Claude Makélélé (French, Retired)

Makélélé was one of the key players in Jose`s Mourinho`s team at Chelsea. This was the team that won the league in 2005 after 50 years of drought. He was the only player that Real Madrid ever regretted selling in the last 20 years. Until 2014, Real Madrid had failed to win any European title since Makélélé's departure in 2003.

# Patrick Vieira (French)

Vieira was the captain of Aresnal's 2004 team. For the record, that was the best team to ever play in the history of the club. It was the only team in 200 years to go 49 games undefeated.

# Nemanja Matić (Serbian)

Matić is one of best three defensive midfielders in all of European soccer. He is the second best tackler in England after Francis Coquelin. Nemanja Matic is at the top of his game right now.

Since he arrived back at Chelsea, he has been the best and most consistent defensive midfielder in the Premier League. Matic may not get the recognitions of Terry, Fabregas and Costa, but he should do. He excels in his role, that's for sure.

It's fair to say that in the last season, 2014/15 he was one of Chelsea's most underappreciated players. There is no doubt in my mind that Matic is the cornerstone of a successful Chelsea club.

As long as he stays on form, then it's my guess that the Blues will be in a good, solid position to keep the Premier League title.

# Francis Coquelin (French)

Many agree that Francis Coquelin is the best defensive midfielder in the Premier League right now (2015). The French midfielder has come a long way since his days as a somewhat part-time fringe player.

He is now one of the most vital cogs in Arsene Wenger's defensive machine. His popularity with fans has gone up in the charts too, thanks to his outstanding performances.

Coquelin is also outperforming many of the other greats, and in several departments. Manchester United's Morgan Schneiderlin is one, and Manchester City's Fernandinho is another. He's also doing better than Chelsea's Nemanja Matic at the present time. Coquelin comes out on top in the number of tackles won; pass completion, duels won, and blocks.

These four players have five special qualities. These are essential qualities, necessary if a midfielder is to make the "perfect tackle." Those qualities are: focus, aggression, anticipation, bravery and positioning. Let's look at each of these in more detail.

# Focus

The first skill is to focus and focus hard. That means you maintain sticky eyes on the ball. It's important that the eyes are on the ball and not the movement of the player's legs or his body.

A great way to develop this skill is by playing lots of air hockey, either on a real table or the computer version. Don't forget, the focus is always on the ball, never the player.

---

# Aggression

The next skill to look at here is aggression. That doesn't mean being nasty or unfair. In this sense, aggression means having the ability to perform hard tackles whenever necessary. It's important to be aggressive in most situations.

That means even if the other player is bigger and stronger than you are. In fact, you need to be aggressive even more so when the opponent is bigger and stronger than you are. You can't worry about getting injured or humiliated.

To be aggressive means to be 100 percent determined and confident of success. To get yourself into this mode you must remove any thoughts from your mind of NOT being able to reach the ball.

Having aggression needs the right mindset. It's all about how you perceive yourself. It's not a simple case of is there any aggression within you, it's more a case of can you let it out when you need it most.

With aggression you are able to go for every ball, every pass and every cross, no matter how hard or rough the play is. With aggression you can take advantage of every mistake and erratic ball that comes into play.

It is only when you have real aggression that you get to set yourself apart from other players. When you can play aggressively, others will see you as a formidable force on the soccer field.

As I said earlier, to be aggressive doesn't mean you're to be nasty or unfair. It's important to put this into perspective. A lot of folks view aggression as feelings of anger or hostility. They associate it to hostile or violent behavior. They are right too, in one sense. But this is not the kind of aggression I'm referring to here.

That is what we call "uncontrolled aggression" and it has no place on the soccer field. What I'm talking about is "controlled aggression," which is not the same thing. It means you have a readiness to attack or confront with force and determination.

The difference here is that you do this in a controlled, yet forceful way. There is no time for good manners or hesitation on the soccer field. This is why you will often need to go in and tackle hard.

## Anticipation

The third essential skill is the ability to anticipate various situations. What this means is that you need to know where the ball is likely to go next. It is your ability to read the situation at the time.

Quite often you will have to first predict where the ball will go before you decide to tackle. This is especially important with slide tackles and intercepting crosses played low to the ground.

# Bravery

To be brave is to play without fear and caution. The braver you are when dealing with situations, the more confident you become in your ability.

A good midfielder has mental and physical toughness, though there are a few exceptions to the physical rule. But he is always brave, even if he lacks in stature.

It's important to point out that being fearless is not the same as being careless. To be brave means you have the courage to go into tough situations, but you also know when not to. It's important to understand the difference. Sometimes, the brave thing to do is to hold back, even when you would sooner get stuck in.

Knowing when to go in and when to hold back is something that will develop with experience. The question you need to ask yourself now is how brave are you.

Are you as brave as you need to be when playing in tough games? Understand that developing bravery has more to do with psychology than physical ability.

# Positioning

It's crucial to position yourself in the right place. That means you choose the perfect launch point from where to perform your slide or tackle. This is an important skill that needs a sensitive decision.

It is something that can only come with experience. Every time you slide too early and fail to make it to the ball you leave behind an empty space. This is a space that your opponent will take advantage of.

Imagine if you're a holding midfielder like Sergio Busquets or Javier Mascherano. If any of these guys make a wrong tackle it causes a lot of upset. If they fail to reach the ball it then creates a one-to-one situation between the attacker and the goalkeeper. That is something you will want to avoid as much as you can.

**Coming up next…**

The quality of your warm up affects the quality of your tackles. Skipping or skimping on a warmup routine is not an option for serious players. In the next chapter, we take a look at what happens if you fail to warm up before a game or practice session.

# 6. Not Warming up Before a Game or Practice Session

The quality of your warm up affects the quality of your tackles. You can be in a lot of trouble whenever you fail to do a proper warm up or skip it altogether. Your ability to stretch your legs to the max and perform great tackles depends on how well you warmed up beforehand.

Even if you are young and supple, that doesn't mean you can skip a warm-up before a practice or game. Warm-ups are necessary and not just done for the sake of it. Those who miss or skimp on warm-ups always pay a price. Let's take a closer look at the two main reasons why it is so important to warm up.

- To prevent injury
- To prepare your physical condition

What this means is that warming up prepares your body for action. Not warming up, on the other hand, means you start the game or practice with an unprepared body.

The result of that makes you more susceptible to injury. It also means you won't be able to perform at your best. These things are most notable in the early minutes of a game or practice session.

To warm up is to reach a level of flexibility that allows your body to handle different situations on the field. Failure to warm up means you're not ready to handle fast, aggressive attacks from the outset.

In other words, you're not in the best physical condition to react as well as you would like to. A typical warming up routine should include the following:

## Stretches

Stretching is a simple yet necessary routine. Begin with 2–4 minutes of light jogging. This warms up your joints by improving blood flow. This alone decreases the chances of getting injured.

After the light jog, perform 20 second stretches for each of your major muscles. These are the quads, hamstrings, calf, upper body, neck and shoulders. Don't stretch to the point where you become fatigued or your muscles start to ache.

Stick to the 20-second rule for each of the muscles, no more. Accompany this with three sets of light jumping (20 seconds each). Once done, you're good to then start warming up with the ball.

## Prepare Your Physical Condition

Start practicing headers, slides and crosses. Do this from different places and at different speeds. Take shots at the goal too, and from different angles. What you're doing here is getting yourself familiar with the game. This ensures you are well-prepared when it's time to play for real.

There's not much to a standard warm-up, but failure to warm up is plain crazy. It can have a negative effect on your ability to play well in those early minutes of the game. Skipping or skimping on a warm-up routine is just not worth the gamble.

Performance aside, you are also vulnerable to injury when you skimp on or skip a warm-up. Believe me, an injury is the last thing in the world you want to happen. Imagine that, skipping a short warm-up resulting in unnecessary pain and discomfort.

Worst still is that it could see you taking months off the field just to recover. Sometimes, depending on the injury, a player never gets back to how he was before an accident.

# Preparing for Different Plays

Here we look at how to prepare for the various tackles you will encounter on the field, starting with the Block Tackle.

## The Block Tackle

- Close the distance and assume a defensive stance.
- Draw your blocking foot and position it sideways.
- Face your opponent, keeping your shoulders squared.
- Move momentum forward and drive the blocking foot through the ball.
- Keep your foot firm as you push the ball forward pass your opponent.
- When you gain possession, try to begin an immediate counterattack.

# The Poke Tackle

- Start by closing the distance and assume the defensive stance.
- Extend your tackling foot.
- Flex your balanced leg.
- Poke the ball with your toes.
- Withdraw your leg to avoid contact with your opponent.
- Chase and regain possession of the ball.

# The Slide Tackle

- Approach from the side. Make the slide on your side and have your arms extended out to the sides for balance.
- Extend your lower leg and have your upper leg flexed at the knee.
- Use the instep of your lower leg to clear the ball away (try to avoid your opponent).
- Jump to your feet and collect the ball whenever possible.

Before you go in for the tackle you need to ask yourself the following questions. There are quite a few of them, but don't worry about the number.

These are things that you will run through your head in nanoseconds, once you become aware of your options, that is.

- What are the potential shooting/passing angles available for the opponent?

- How can I contain this attacker and cover as many angles as possible?
- What are all the passing options available to this attacker (the ball holder)?
- How should I position myself so that I'm able to catch the next pass or cross before it reaches the man I'm marking?
- How to balance between keeping an eye on the man I'm marking and covering for my next teammate?
- When should I stick to my position and when should I leave it?
- What do I want from this situation and how can I force the ball holder to follow my plan of action?
- When should I interfere and how?
- Where am I from the penalty area? Where am I from the goal area/goal line? And where am I from my teammates (especially the nearest of them)?
- What's the next possible scenario for the ball holder to follow?
- What should I do if he gets past me?
- Which is my opponent's dominant foot (the one he uses most)? Which is my opponent's weakest foot (the one he uses least)? How can I best position myself so that I force him to use his weak foot?

They say that soccer only has two types of player, the goalkeeper and everyone else. But whatever your role is, each player needs to have different skills.

And because he has different roles he takes on different positions at various times. When you know how to position yourself well, you then get to make a huge difference to the way you perform.

# 7. Not Having Good Communication with Your Teammates

It doesn't always matter if there's not a lot of communication going on between the strikers. It is important, however, to have good communication between you and your teammates if you are the Regista.

This is because it's your job to control the pace of the game. You have to distribute roles and guide your teammates throughout the entire 90 minutes. The only way you can do any of this is with good, effective communication.

Let's look at some situations where good communication is essential on the field.

---

# Free Kicks

A goalkeeper has to communicate with his teammates when setting up his defensive wall. This is not an option but a must-do. Good communication applies to both direct and indirect free kicks. It is something that is important for all concerned.

The aim here is to block all possible shooting opportunities for the one taking the free kick. A well-positioned wall also helps the keeper to maintain a good view for the ball. Any wrong positioning from you while standing in the wall can put your team in a lot of danger.

---

# Leading Counter Attacks

In most cases, it is midfielders who start a counter attack. They either recover the ball near the penalty area or they receive it at the defensive line. In these situations you run with the ball and use passes to connect between the defense and the attacking line.

The only way to execute a counter attack with any success is through effective communication. You need to practice these scenarios before the games.

It's the only way you can get to know how your team will react during a real counter attack. Observe where they prefer the passes from and how.

A quick and effective way to communicate is with the eyes. Reading a player's eyes, and other forms of body language, lets you play a fast and accurate game.

A quick glance between you and your teammates should be enough to tell you where he will pass the ball to (or vice versa).

You then move into position based on your silent communication. It might sound difficult, but it's not. All you have to do is get used to reading the intentions of your teammates, and them with you, using glances.

Silent communication with the eyes, along with other forms of body language, can be effective like you wouldn't believe.

# Facing Counter Attacks

None of the midfielders faces a direct counter attack, except when playing as a DM. Good communication and the distribution of roles between the two central midfielders is crucial. It plays an important role at defusing a counter attack.

A typical counter attack consists of three attackers facing two defenders/midfielders. The problems occur when one of the two defending players makes a wrong move.

He might do this by advancing and then failing to reach the ball in time in his attempt to intercept it. In other words, he fails to react quicker than the opposition.

There is only one way to recover the ball from a strong counter attack. It can only come about when both defenders take the right positions. That position is between the rival passer (the one with the ball) and the attacking player nearest to you.

But even if you are both in perfect positions, none of it will come to much unless you have good communication. You need to decide which one of you will go after the ball, and who will be responsible for the coverage.

Anytime you fail to distribute roles or lose communication you're in big trouble. The ball will either end up in your goal or at least create a situation that puts your side in serious danger.

# Any Change in the Attacking Formation of the Opposite Team

This can be a smart move, which accounts for why it happens a lot in soccer. Note that changes in an opponent's formation can come about fast and without notice.

When you play in the middle you are the first to notice any changes in the opposite team's formation. If they're sneaky and smart, you may not notice at all, at least not right away. The reason why changes in formation can be so effective is because they can disrupt your strategy.

For example, you have gotten used to playing a certain way against certain players. Then all of a sudden, you find yourself pitted against a different player(s).

He may have a total different approach and style to what you had gotten used to. When this happens, the rival side gets the upper hand.

Changes might be with new substitutions or a couple of players changing roles/sides. They might introduce an extra player to provide fresh coverage in the middle. Maybe they put in a new, fast winger to play against your team's slowest full back.

Or it could be a new attacker who relies on shooting from outside the penalty area. As a team leader, your job is to notify your teammates of any changes in the rival side's formation. If you don't, then they can't prepare themselves.

# Switching Positions

In a lot of cases, the CM or CAM has the freedom to move either alongside the two penalty areas or on the flanks. To do this he needs to switch roles with wingers, and sometimes attackers. Of course, whether this happens or not depends upon the game conditions at the time.

Whatever you do, never make any such changes without letting the others know of you plan. Effective communication is essential in these situations. If you fail to communicate, then your plan will backfire. If you communicate well, then you're in with a chance to mess with the rival defenders and surprise them.

Get familiar with the roles of all your players. Understand why they sometimes switch roles and change their actions.

When you can do this you get to understand just how important communication is. That in turn will make you better at communicating with your teammates.

# Distributing Roles

In free kicks and set pieces good communication is essential. Defensive players, including defenders, tall DMs and tall attackers, really do need to communicate. They need to decide who marks who and be totally clear about their roles.

The best way for this to happen is to decide who does what before the game begins. Having said that, there will be occasions where the rival side has made changes in in their team's tactics.

When this happens, it might be necessary to change your role inside the penalty area. It all depends on how things materialize during the time.

## When Not Covering Their Position

All wingers should support the back players on their side. This will either be a left back (LB) or a right back (RB). It's even more important if this left or right back is the weakest link of your defensive line.

This means you have to support and communicate with him at all times. Your lines of communication should be open anytime you notice him making a mistake. This could be errors with either coverage or distributing the ball.

# 8. Not Adapting to Changes in the Playing Strategy

Anytime a player from your team gets sent off things can end up quite messy. Your coach will have to make changes in the team's playing strategy too. When this happens he starts by making a substitution. He will enter a defensive player if the man sent off was a back or a defensive midfielder "a stopper."

The gaps between all the three lines of your team (the attack, the midfield and the defense) need closing. This is most important for the space between the defenders and the midfielders.

# When Leading the Score

When your team is leading in the score you should wait before you make your next moves. When the rival side starts looking for a goal, then it's time for you spring into action. When you do, it's important to put your focus on moving the ball to the front as quick as you can.

You can do this by using either long or short passes. The opponents will be attacking with full force in these situations.

When that happens, they will leave empty spaces behind their players. That means it will take a lot longer for them to recover from the attacking to the defensive position.

You may prefer to keep the ball moving around to waste time, but don't do that. Attack is your best defensive option here.

Killing the game with a late goal will make your job much easier. It's certainly easier than killing time, waiting for the ref to blow the final whistle.

So any time you see the rival side making a desperate attempt to score, prepare to attack. Remember to always move the ball from the back to the front, and as fast as possible.

# When Falling Behind in the Score

There will be times when you need to move and try to score a goal as your opponents outnumber you. What action you take in these situations will depend on the position you have in the midfield.

If you're a defensive midfielder, you will have to play at the center line. This will require you to double your efforts to make up for the man short.

It also means you need to stay close to your center back so that you can close more gaps when need be. The things you reply on most in a situation like this are your determination and aggression.

If you are an attacking midfielder, you will have to avoid playing long balls. This is because the other team will be compact near their penalty area.

To beat the other team's defensive, you have to move the ball fast. You will do this using short passes and your dribbling skills.

You must not be tempted to shoot the ball from outside the penalty area. It will more than likely end up as a wasted shot if you do.

By this time, the rival players would have closed, or be closing, most shooting gaps. The only time to take a shot from outside the penalty area is if you have a golden opportunity to score.

It's also a good idea to pass your corners to the nearest teammate. It's often better if he sends the cross instead of you.

This is one of those moves that can force the other team to change their defensive formation. When that happens, it can work nicely in your favor.

# 9. Not Applying Pressure on the Referee

One thing you should never be afraid to do, and that is to put pressure on the referee. I would say always put pressure on the ref when you need to. So how can you go about this? Well, you can ask for fouls and you can protest against any of his decisions that seem unfair.

You will always want to pressure him if you feel he's favoring the other side over your team. Believe me, this is something that happens at times. Make sure to question his decisions whenever a foul is in doubt. Also question his decisions whenever he makes a mistake.

And always ask the ref to defend you if there is an opponent who is getting a little too aggressive. If any of your protests to the ref fall on deaf ears, then it's time to take things up a notch.

You do this by rallying your teammates together so that you can surround the referee and talk to him as a group. This tactic is especially useful if your side feels he's favoring the other team by his decisions.

We're now going to look at a couple of teams that are masters at putting pressure on referee. They are F.C. Barcelona and Atletico Madrid. These are two of the most successful soccer teams around at the moment.

Players of both sides are so good at pressuring refs that you have to see it to believe it. In fact, any game between these two sides becomes an out and out nightmare for any referee taking that game. Let's look at a couple of examples of how they do this, starting with F.C. Barcelona.

# Case 1: F.C Barcelona

As you know, F.C. Barcelona is a team with a lot of talented players. Four of the best are perhaps Messi, Neymar, Luis Suarez and Andres Iniesta. Because there is so much talent in one team, it makes them a formidable side to play against. In fact, it places huge pressure on any side that challenges them.

Other teams often feel that the only way to beat the superstars is to use excessive aggression. That means they go in with a lot of hard tackles and barging. This is obviously a threat to the Barcelona players.

It means they have more chance of suffering injuries than players of other teams. Because of this, they feel that they need extra protection. Well, the only person who can provide them with that is the referee of course.

The Barcelona situation all began with their massively successful team of 2007. It was a time when they emerged with their Tiki-Taka playing style. Their high scoring rates became a problem for rival teams.

Frustrated players of other sides would get frustrated and agitated by Barcelona's success. Because of this, they would start to get more aggressive in their playing style; way more aggressive than is normal.

This rough approach set a precedent for anyone up against the Barcelona side. Ronaldinho and Messi in particular were having a tough time of it all.

The Barca players got to the point where they couldn't take it anymore. They realized that there was only one way to deal with this type of severe aggression. Their solution was to complain to the ref, and complain hard.

They knew their complaints would be futile if they approached him one player at a time. So they would gather around him in a group. Actually, it's more a case of gang up, than gather. So they would pressure him to stop their opponents from using undue force against them.

They wouldn't rest until they got what they wanted either. Hounding the ref became a common practice. They would approach him with every single tackle made against any of them. They would even approach him when the tackle wasn't that aggressive.

As a result of this tactic they gained the protection they needed, but that's not all they got. Because they became so good at forcing the ref to keep a watchful eye on their opponents, something else happened in their favor. Have you guessed yet?

Their own work on the field became even easier. Now that referees spend so much time looking out for foul play in the teams against Barcelona, they spend less time watching them. Because of this, Barcelona gets away with things they wouldn't normally get away with.

Messi is an international treasure, all referees know that. That means he needs extra safety and protection. Because of who he is, he's vulnerable to all kinds of aggressive behavior. But any opponents know that refs are always looking out for soccer's Golden Boy.

This is good news for Messi but not such good news for his rivals. In a lot of cases, other players don't dare go in too hard against Messi. They fear that making a hard tackle against this guy might get them booked or even sent off. In other words, Messi's challengers will often pussyfoot around him to avoid hassle.

You don't have to take my word for this. Check out YouTube vids for yourself. You will find a plethora of clips with incidents for Barcelona players. Look out in particular for the likes of Dani Alves. Look too for their defensive midfielder, Sergio Busquets. These guys often deceive the referee with fake dives and fake injuries.

Many of these incidents result in fouls for their side and bookings for those playing against them. Since all refs are now programmed to protect Barcelona players, the team gets away with all sorts. This is a classic case of whatever brings results gets repeated.

## Case 2: Atletico Madrid

OK, so the second team that has become expert at pressuring referees is Atletico Madrid. Their story started in more recent times, around 2011. It was at a time when Diego Simeone took his new position as the head coach, with the team he used to play for back in the 1990s.

Simeone was the Argentine captain for more than eight years. Everyone knows him, or knows of him, on the international soccer circuit. He is someone renowned for his high spirits.

This is a man who has a real winning mindset. Some will say his enthusiastic style is all about bully-boy tactics and aggression. Well, whether you like him or not, this is a man who gets results, no one can argue with that.

Simeone didn't waste any time once he arrived at Madrid. He took everything he knew about winning and poured it all into the hearts and minds of his players.

It worked too. He managed to turn the Atletico Madrid squad into real warriors; guys who would stop at nothing to triumph. Even if they had to play rough soccer to win, they would do whatever it took.

Any kind of excessive rough play in soccer can lead to trouble. In fact, it will get you booked a lot, that's if the ref catches you. That's not good for your career or the reputation of your team. Even so, it has to be said that Atletico Madrid became a pretty rough side. Because of this, Simeone and his assistants needed to protect themselves from referees.

The reason was because most refs were, and still are, on the constant lookout for any misbehavior from the team.

So they decided back then to adopt a new tactic, and Simeone knew just what to do. Atletico Madrid began to take the "let's pressure the referee" approach to their games. They thought it would be a good way to avoid getting red and yellow cards.

Did it work?

I think you already know the answer to this. Watch any of Atletico Madrid's games and you will see for yourself. Note how the players gang up on the refs all the time.

They protest after just about every serious decision made by a referee. You can find them talking to him, shouting at him, and debating every decision he makes.

They will also remind him of every single mistake he ever made during the game. It's fair to say that Atletico Madrid's players have become a ref's worst nightmare.

They can get a referee to the point where he may even give one of them a borderline foul. He might do this even if it's not really warranted.

Or he may avoid giving any of the team a yellow or red card. He does this just to save himself from grief and mind fatigue. The Atletico Madrid players don't only pressure the ref either. They will happily bully the linesman as well, if need be.

As you read about these teams you might be thinking to yourself that these tactics are unfair. Well, soccer does have set rules, and everyone expects fair play and clean games, in a perfect world. But this is not a perfect world and soccer is a rough and tumble sport. So it means teams and team players will often do whatever it takes to win.

If they find a winning formula, they won't worry too much about whether it's the right thing to do or not, especially if there's a good chance of getting away with it. The only thing that matters is whether they get to produce results.

The higher up the leagues you go, the more pressure there is to triumph. So there's not always room for pleasantries or fair play in competitive soccer.

# 10. You Lose Your Temper Easy

Not all players' manage to stay calm during a high tempo, high pressured game. There are some though, who seem to lose their temper at the slightest upset. It might be entertaining to fans, but is not helpful to the one having the tantrum.

Anyone who loses their temper during a game shows signs of weakness, not strength. There may be times when it's justified to get upset about something. But there is no such thing as a justifiable angry outburst on the field. It's even less acceptable when that outburst leads to a physical confrontation, or fight.

The one thing you should try to do when you play soccer is to stay calm. Just know that letting off steam damages your game, your reputation, and that of your team. It never wins anything, but there is always plenty to lose. Some teams, and some players on certain teams, are great at pushing the buttons of rival players.

In fact, it's a part of their game strategy. The best thing you can do in these situations is to not take the bait. Be especially prepared to keep your cool when playing against pushy teams. There are always a few of them that are notorious for being brash, aggressive or insulting.

From time to time you will face rival players who will attempt to wind you up. It's nothing personal; it's all part of their mental game plan. They do it with the sole purpose to intimidate you. If they are successful and you get agitated, then your performance declines as a result.

If you have an emotional outburst you might even get a yellow or red card, depending on your reaction. When that happens, it's one nil to the tormentor because his tactic has worked.

Note this important fact: you are unlikely to mix bad temper with good performance. Because of this, no club in their right mind will want to invest in any player who doesn't know how to control his temper. Some teams do have such players in their squads.

This is not because they welcome them, of course. It's because they were unaware that player was prone to hissy fits when they signed him up. Such players spell trouble on the game field. Furthermore, they become unpopular with the other players and the fans. Whenever there's a bad egg in the team, it can damage team moral, and that's never a good thing. In short, anyone who cannot control their temper on the field is bad news.

If you are someone who has a short fuse, then this is something you will need to address. The best way you can stay calm on the field is to prepare. In other words, expect that there may be people or situations that could trigger your temper.

Knowing that something might happen, and having a plan to deal with it if it does, is your best defense. OK, let's look at how a player might try to fire you up the wrong way.

It is in your opponent's best interest if you lose your cool. He knows it will have a negative effect on the way you play. This is the reason he will try to upset you. He may try to taunt you at first, whenever you're within earshot of him. He will make jokes and perhaps even throw insults your way, mocking all your attempts to defeat him.

His only goal is to distract you; he's trying to get you lose focus. If he can get you riled by his taunting, it means that whatever he's doing or saying is working. This means he's likely to continue with his plan.

And if he's really lucky, he can get you to respond with an aggressive reaction. If the ref sees you lashing out in a fit of temper, he will give you a yellow or even a red card. If that happens, your team becomes outnumbered and it's a win for the striker. He's done a great job, as far as he's concerned.

Expect these things to happen from time to time, because they will. And make sure you have a plan to deal with them when they do. You are then in a better position to make things backfire on the one who is trash-talking you.

Your best response in these situations is not to reciprocate with more of the same. All that does is show the opponent that he's getting to you. You best response is to ignore him as best you can. And the best way to do this is to not make eye contact, or respond verbally.

Yes, he's still there and yes he's still annoying. But you should feed off his intimidation tactics. Get angry, if you have to, but don't show it in a way the one doing the taunting hopes for. Channel your anger or annoyance into your game, not your opponent.

Play with as much determination and skill as you can muster. There is no better way to have his intimidation tactics backfire than to ignore him and play great soccer. Let's look at a real example to illustrate the point.

# Joey Barton (Bad Boy Joe)

Here we will use Joey Barton as a perfect example. You are about see the problems that can materialize from displaying a bad temper on the soccer field.

Barton has heart, he is a real fighter on the field, and he has great defensive skills. Those are his good points. But there's a darker side to this midfielder.

Any attacker who plays against Barton can stir up his anger using the smallest of taunts. Seriously, it doesn't take much at all to get Barton to show his aggressive side. Rival strikers know this, and use it to their advantage.

Barton is the good boy bad boy of soccer. He played for Newcastle United. He won the English premier league with Manchester City. But his career started to take a turn for the worse after he became a symbol of bad temper and aggressive behavior.

His outburst became more and more frequent and his career began to go south as a consequence. He went on to play for the below average team, Queens Park Rangers, which he relegated.

He's now ending his career with Burnley F.C., in the second division. None of this had to happen; he allowed it to happen by not working on his temper tantrums.

Barton would fight with anyone who pushed his buttons. He had fights with players from Arsenal, Manchester City, Liverpool and Blackburn Rovers. He once punched the Norwegian winger, Morten Gamst Pedersen, in the chest.

He gave Ryan Babel a bleeding nose. And he dropped his shorts to expose two peachy buttocks to the home fans of Norwich City. This happened after he got sent off the field. The list of bad incidents goes on and on, which is more than can be said for his career.

## Pepe (Képler Laveran Lima Ferreira)

The central defender, Pepe, is yet another example of a player who loses his temper too easily on the field. In fact, Pepe can be way too aggressive for his own good. For the record, Pepe is a Portuguese professional.

He plays for the Spanish club Real Madrid, and the Portuguese national team. I'm, sure that both of these clubs wished he played for someone other than them. It can't be much fun wondering when he will blow up next, or what he might do when he does.

I would say that Pepe is one of the most aggressive, bad tempered defensive players of the last 20 years. His good point is that he's also one of the most skilled defenders in the world right now. This will be the only reason why he's still hanging on to his career.

Pepe's major disadvantage, without any question of doubt, is his inability to control his rage. He can snap real easy, and that makes him both unpredictable and damaging to the game. It doesn't take much at all to get him all hot and bothered.

It might be a verbal taunt from an opponent, or the game just isn't going his way. If Pepe's not happy, everyone around him gets to know about it. To say the guy has a short fuse is a gross understatement.

I can recall one incident that was particularly nasty. It happened during a game in the Spanish league. The attacker playing against Pepe tried to fake a dive inside the goal area.

This might not be fair play, but it is something soccer players do at times nonetheless. They do it in the hope that the ref will award them with a penalty.

Well, that act was enough to trigger Pepe's fiery temper. He booted that player hard in the legs, and followed that with a swift kick to his back as he went to the ground. If that wasn't enough, he then went back to that player a few seconds later.

This time he kicked him again and grabbed his hair. He then tried to start a fight with the player's teammates as they rallied around to defend their buddy. It was quite a scene, and an ugly one at that.

Pepe got a red card for his unacceptable behavior, which only upset him further. He then went on to trash-talk the referee and the lines man. The whole thing was just awful.

It took the beauty out of an otherwise beautiful game. Some would argue that Pepe is not just hot-tempered but completely unhinged. This explains why he's earned the nickname, Pepe the Assassin.

The incident above didn't just stop with a red card either. Pepe got a ban from playing for eight months. As you might have guessed, this caused a lot of problems for his team. They couldn't replace him either, since the transfer market had already ended.

It's sad to say that this incident was not a one-off. Pepe's aggressiveness is notorious. His bad behavior reared its ugly head again soon after he returned from his long ban.

He gave the French left back, Aly Cissokho, a martial arts kick in one game. This happened in the Champions league with Lyon Vs Real Madrid.

Pepe also has an aggressive attitude toward Barcelona players in general. Because of this, he's become a real pain in the neck for Real Madrid.

Whenever these two teams play against each other, the referees have to be extra vigilant. They know that Pepe could snap at any moment.

Because of this, the refs have to protect Barcelona players against his violent outbursts. This added tension sometimes means there are unfair, mistaken decisions made by the refs.

It's not surprising either; I mean, the poor guys must be on tenterhooks for the entire game. Heck, refs have enough to do managing a soccer game as it is. Having to babysit players with temper tantrums is the last thing they need.

# Felipe Melo VS Arjen Roben

The Brazilian, Felipe Melo, was once one of the best defensive midfielders in the world. I say was because he's lost it all now.

This is as a result of his extremely aggressive behaviors in critical game situations. Let's look at the 2010 World Cup when Brazil met the Netherlands, as one example.

This incident happened in the knockout stage. Despite making his team's only assist in the game, Melo went on to score an own goal for Netherlands.

He then went on to stamp on Arjen Robben's leg and almost broke it. He got a direct red card for that. Brazil was then knocked out of the World Cup.

It's no surprise that Felipe Melo never made it into the Brazilian national team again after that incident.

## Diego Costa Vs Gabriel Paulista

Let's now look at a situation from the North London Derby between Chelsea and Arsenal. During the game, Chelsea's striker, Diego Costa, hit Arsenal`s defender, Laurent Koscielny, three times.

Everyone knows Costa for his sneaky, pushy style, and the way he plays against the rules. Because of this, to see him misbehave is never a surprise.

In the incident above, neither the referee nor the linesman saw what had happened. What happened next though, is interesting.

Koscielny's partner, Gabriel Paulista, saw the incident with his teammate. He then went over to Costa and picked a fight with him. The ref saw this and had no choice but to give both of them a yellow card.

Just 20 seconds later, Costa then went over to Paulista and began cursing him. He then hit Paulista from behind when the ref wasn't looking, and waited for him to respond.

His plan was to throw himself to the ground the moment the ref turned to look in their direction. If his plan worked, the referee would have no choice but to send the Arsenal defender off for bad behavior. So did it work?

Yes, it did, it worked like a charm. Gabriel Paulista got sent off and Costa continued to play and help lead his team to a 2-0 win against their rivals.

The reason to highlight the above account is twofold. The first is to illustrate how trying to be a hero can backfire. In short, stay out of fights that don't involve you.

At the very least, stay out of fights while the game is on. The second point I want to make is the importance of knowing how to control your temper. Paulista wasn't the one who Costa hit.

Instead of playing the super hero, he could have just notified the referee of the incident. But no, he had to go and try to sort things out himself.

You might at first think his actions were gallant, but it was actually a stupid decision. Because of his misconduct, his team then had to play the rest of the game with 10 players instead of 11. That's not what you might call a smart outcome.

# Zinedine Zidane: The Worst Ending for a Great Player

Let's look now at an incident between Zinedine Zidane and Marco Materazzi. It happened in the 2006 World Cup final game where France's Zinedine Zidane was playing his last ever game.

Alas, it was not to be a fond farewell for the French midfielder. In fact, he actually got sent off for misconduct.

What he did was head-butt Italy's Marco Materazzi's, and hard too, right in his chest. It was in retaliation to Materazzi trash-talking him. I don't condone the act by any means, but Materazzi was successful at pressuring Zidane. He got him so riled that he just snapped. The attacking midfielder was then out of the game.

This is exactly what Materazzi had hoped would happen. How upset had he made Zidane with his trash-talking?

Well, let's just say that Zidane said he would rather die than apologize to Marco Materazzi. That's a pretty successful taunt on Materazzi's part.

If Zidane had kept calm and remained focused on the game, the outcome might have been quite different. He could have actually helped France win their second World Cup title. But he didn't.

He will probably spend the rest of his life blaming himself for destroying their chances. Remember, if you ever get angry, channel that anger into your game, not the opponent taunting you.

# 11. Not Perfecting Your Decision Making Process

Soccer players often face a lot of decisions and options during a game. The skill is to choose the right decision for the situation at the time. And because of the pace of soccer, they have to make quick decisions followed by fast actions.

As mentioned earlier in the book, physical skills alone are not enough to make you a great player. Of course you have fantastic dribbling skills, but without having the right mental approach they won't get you far. So you have to perfect your decision making process.

Your game will skyrocket when you can couple the right decisions with skillful actions. Get to do this on a regular basis and you move up to the next level in your soccer career. Let's look at how you can hone in on your decision making skills.

There is a simple process that you can follow which will help you develop your decision making. It consists of three basic stages. These stages are: the bulking stage, the filtering stage and the blocking stage. OK, we will now go through each of these in turn.

# The Bulking Stage

The only thing you need to be aware of with the bulking stage is yourself. By that, I mean you need to become aware of what you do and how you think. A lot of what we do comes from intuition. In other words, once we have learned to do something, we do it without too much conscious thought.

Well, the bulking stage is where you have to consciously think about what you do and why. This is to be a fact finding mission. So just continue to play as you do normally, only for the next few weeks you are to note everything down.

We all make some mistakes, but we don't always take a lot of notice of them at the time. If you make a small error on the field, chances are you will press on with the game and think no more of it. From now on though, you don't let anything escape, you have to write it all down.

It is only when you can identify flaws in your game that you can work at fixing them. There can be no solutions until you first know what the problem areas are. So in this bulking stage, you take a lot of notes. Don't just write down the areas you fall short on either. Also make notes on what you do well.

## The Point of Bulking

The whole point of bulking is to build a complete picture of your game. The more mistakes you identify, the more you get to work on.

To build a complete personal profile you need to play in lots of different situations. See if you can take on different roles.

Start by trying different types of passes. Then move on to different types of shots. Don't forget to note down your thoughts and actions once your training or game is over. You're not looking to improve at this stage; you're just getting everything down on paper as it is. Play against different types of attackers/defenders.

This should include the fast, the strong, the talented and the pushy. Note down how you fare in each situation. The more teams and players you get to play against the better it is for you.

This way you get to experience more tactics and playing styles. You are on a mission to discover every single strength and weakness you have. This data is going to be invaluable to you later on, and I do mean invaluable.

So remember, the most important thing here is to try different things. You want to expose yourself to as many new plays and situations as you can.

Keep your experiences written either on paper or on a text file. Once you get home from training, or after a game, take some time out to write stuff down. Do it as soon as you can, while it's still fresh in your mind.

Make notes of where you played well along with any mistakes you made. Also put down what, if anything, you could have done differently. The more you put down, the more valuable this stage will be to you.

## The Filtering Stage

The next stage is the filtering stage. This is where you gather all the data you have written down over the previous weeks. It's now time to turn all those notes into a single manual. What you want to do here is get it all organized into some kind of methodical order.

Separate the good play from the bad. If you have been precise in your note taking, it should all make sense when you start to reread this stuff.

It will include notes like: When "X" happened I should have done "Y." And, when dealing with "A" it would have been better to do "C" rather than "B."

You job here is to filter all your data. Separate it so that you get a complete profile of your game. This includes the good, the not so good, and the useless.

Once you have a few weeks or months of data, you will begin to notice obvious patterns in your game. I can promise you this: by putting your game down on paper, you will learn more about yourself and the way you perform than talking about it ever could.

## The Not Thinking Stage

This is the action stage. It is where you don't think you just do. This is the time where you apply your notes from the filtering stage into positive actions.

You are no longer writing stuff down or analyzing it. The theory part is over now. Before you enter this third stage, you should have identified all flaws in the way you play.

You will also know of any skills that are just average, and that could also use some improvements. Moreover, you should have the solutions down too, so that you can work at fixing stuff. You can remedy some areas of your game real easy; you might just need you to change your approach.

Other areas will need you to work at improving existing skills. You may even find that you have to learn some new things from scratch. The point is that you now understand what you're good at. You also know what needs work, and what, if anything, needs removing altogether.

Many years ago, when I first worked on these stages, I found out a lot about the way I played soccer. One example is how I often wasted a few moments by following the path of at a crossed ball through the air. Once I had identified this pattern, the fix was easy.

I just started to run toward the ball every time from then on. This allowed me to reach the ball before the player I was marking got to it. That tiny shift in the way I responded to these balls made a big difference to my game. I also noticed how I would often forget about the guy I was marking and stray away from my position.

Again, my game improved when I started to give full focus to my designated role. These things and more besides changed my mindset, my attitude, and the way I played soccer. It was all good, and a very worth wile exercise.

The great thing about soccer is that it's often the little tweaks in the way we play that can make the biggest difference to the outcome of our game. But before we can make any changes, big or small, we first have to know what we need to do.

This is why the three-stepped approach is so useful. This is a fast paced game that needs quick thinking followed by fast actions.

So I urge you to work through the three stages outlined in this chapter. As long as you do it right, and follow through with positive action, great things will come to pass. This is something I can guarantee.

# 12. You Hold the Ball for Too Long

Can you guess what one of the biggest mistakes is that a midfielder makes, regardless of his position? It is to hold on to the ball for way too long.

Except in certain situations, which I will explain later, the ball needs to move to the front, and move fast.

You and the ball should always be approaching the other goal. Your job is to keep that ball away from your own goal at all costs.

Anyone can make a game unnecessarily complex, but only the real pros know how to play simple soccer. By the way, don't confuse simple with easy, because they are not the same thing.

Watch how Pep Guardiola reacts from the sideline when any of his players in Bayern Munich holds the ball for too long. He's not a happy-chappy, that's for sure.

The way we play soccer today has changed a lot. Or at least when you compare it to how we used to play it has. In modern soccer, games have become more tactical. For example, many teams nowadays tend to "Park the Bus." Wikipedia best explains what that means:

*Parking the bus: expression used when all the players on a team play defensively, usually when the team is intending to draw the game or defending a narrow margin. The term was coined by Chelsea F.C. manager, Jose Mourinho, referring to Tottenham Hotspur F.C. during a game against Chelsea in 2004.*

So it's an expression used to describe the tactical game played by Jose Mourinho's teams. It means to focus mainly on defense and not to concede any goals under any circumstances. The term suggests putting a bus in front of the goal to block any balls, figuratively speaking of course.

What does this mean to you, as a modern midfielder? Well, you should be able to move the ball as fast as possible. You need to make good use of the few minutes you have with that ball during a game.

According to statistics, a player can't expect to have the ball for more than three minutes on average during an entire game.

# When to Slow Down the Game

When a team is under constant attack by the opposition for five or more minutes, a good Regista or DM will try to keep the ball in and around his domain.

He will typically pass the ball on to more secure areas on the field. He does this so that his teammates have an opportunity to take a few breaths and recompose themselves.

# Before the End of the Game

The best way to waste time is to hold on to the ball rather than put it into competitive play. This is a tactic that's used a lot, especially with the team that's leading in the score.

In situations like these, the rival side will be desperate to score before the end of the game. Two things to note here: the first is to not let the referee catch you deliberately wasting time.

You have to be smart and subtle about this, so that it's not overly obvious. The second thing you should be aware of is to never hold on to the ball in your penalty area. To do that is just inviting trouble.

The best place to send the ball is toward the left and left flanks. You can waste time when the ball goes out for a corner or a throw-in. Here you can get the ball back, or at least prevent the other side from retaking it.

Whenever you lose the ball, it's easier to apply pressure near the side lines. Don't ever be afraid to send the ball out to a throw—in if that's the best thing to do at the time.

# 13. Choosing Beautiful Soccer on Defusing Attacks – for DMs and CMs

Another big mistake many defensive midfielders make is to err on the side of caution. What this means is that they try to play the ball themselves in tricky situations.

So they hold on to the ball, rather than risk losing it by moving it on. This is more likely to happen with younger guys and amateurs, more so than professionals.

You might be wondering why opting to play it safe is a mistake. The problem is that the safe way is not as safe as these players think. When under attack, with few "safe" options to pass the ball on, the DM tries to play the ball himself.

He thinks that sending the on its way is the worst of two bad choices, so he keeps hold of it. He's wrong about that, and here's why I say this.

When the player has a lot of pressure by one or more opponents, there's a really good chance he will lose the ball. But he feels there are no safer options so he tries anyway.

In these situations, he is still better off passing the ball to the nearest player or sending a long ball towards the opposite side. He's even better off sending the ball to a throw-in than he is challenging the attacker(s) alone.

Unless you're a winger, you will find yourself facing counter attacks. Other times you have to create cover for your defensive teammates. To do any of these things well, you have to lose the idea of hogging the ball and doing your own thing.

Your role requires a tough decisive player. It's a role where your first major skill will be defusing and shutting down the rival team's attacks. You have to do this before the ball even reaches the defensive line.

This all means you have to be comfortable with clearing the ball, and not look for ways to hold on to it. For a stopper, safety always come before attacking.

# Super Mascherano

Barcelona won four major trophies in the 2014/2015 season. These were the Spanish league, the Champions league, the UEFA Super cup and the Copa Del Rey cup. A lot of these victories came about because of the performance of their offensive trio.

That trio was Leo Messi, Neymar Jr., and Luis Suarez. Barcelona didn't triumph only because of these three star players; it was not just a three-man show. These victories could only happen because of the efforts of their defensive midfielder, Javier Mascherano.

Mascherano is an Argentine icon, known for his excellent leadership skills. He helped lead the Argentine national team to the final of the World Cup in 2014 and the final of Copa America in 2015. Mascherano can play well either as a defensive midfielder or central defender. This is something that makes him a real asset to Barcelona.

His main role is defensive midfielder, but he adapts very well to other defensive roles too. Whatever defensive position Mascherano plays, he always performs with impressive skill.

In the 2014/2015 season mentioned above, anytime a player from the back line got injured, Mascherano would be the one to fill the gap, no problem at all.

Mascherano is a guy who plays a simple game. In fact, he plays his defensive midfielder role by the book. He never looks for style or seeks his own glory in any situation.

As far as he's concerned, it's always the team that comes first. So when it comes to defusing an attack he focuses only on destroying the opponent's passes.

He will do whatever it takes to keep his team safe, and he does a great job at it too. If he has to send the ball to the outside, then he will do so without a moment's hesitation. Mascherano's formula is both classic and super focused. It's simple but it's not easy, yet because of his skill he makes it look easy. He takes the right position, plays with aggression, and keeps the ball away. That's it, it's what they expect of him, and so that's what he delivers. Simple in theory, a lot harder in practice, but he does a fantastic job more often than not.

Watch Mascherano play and you will see the simplicity in his style. Note how he positions himself in the center.

He will be somewhere between the ball and the player receiving it. Or he might take a ready–to–run position, behind the player who's waiting to receive the ball. He does this with impressive skill.

When the time is right, he springs into action. You can see him surprise and outrun the player he was behind just moments before. Timing is crucial in these situations.

You have to move the second the ball leaves the passer's foot, not a moment too soon or too late. Once Mascherano reaches the ball, he clears it away without too much lag. This is classic defending.

If Mascherano feels in trouble or is unable to direct the ball to a teammate safely, he does not try to hold onto it. In these situations, he sends it to the outside, that's it. He does this without hesitating because he knows it's the best option for the situation.

Again, it's classic defending. And if he doesn't send the ball to the outside, he will kick it as hard as he can toward the other team's side.

His main concerns, which should be yours too, is to kill the attack. Killing the attack, to him, is definitely more important than trying to look good.

Javier Mascherano is the beast behind Barcelona's beautiful game. No one will dispute that he gives the team balance, both on and off the field.

# 14. Not Trying to Play in Different Roles on the Field

Modern soccer requires a modern approach, and a more flexible style of play. The more flexible a player is to different game plans, the higher his price tag.

In short, the more he can do, the more chance there is that he will find his way into bigger and better teams. All the big coaches look for flexibility in a player nowadays. The geniuses of the coaching field expect nothing less.

This is especially the case when there are big bucks involved. Take the coaches Pep Guardiola, Jose Mourinho and Carlo Ancelotti. These guys are real fussy when choosing new players.

They look for a player (regardless of their official positions) who can take on different roles. These coaches even look for goalkeepers who can adapt to their different game plans. It's true, some keepers are able to play like an eleventh field player when the need arises.

If you want a good example of a flexible goalie, look no further than Manuel Neuer. What he does for the German national team, as well as his own team Bayern Munich, goes above and beyond the call of duty. They don't call Neuer "The Sweeper Keeper" for nothing.

Because of his ability to excel outside the goalkeeping role, Neuer's price tag is high. In fact, it's at least 20 million dollars above other professional goalkeepers.

So what can he do, what is it that makes Neuer so valuable? Well, aside from being phenomenal at keeping his goal safe, he also knows how to play crosses.

He's adept too at creating effective counter attacks. He can also play as a sweeper or Libero. He can predict and intercept the majority of through passes and long balls played behind his defensive line.

He really is exceptional, and he's also quite rare. There are many great goalkeepers around, but none are quite as impressive and Neuer. This is why he demands such a high price tag.

If you want proof of his skills, watch Neuer's performance with Germany against Algeria. This was the game in the last Brazilian World Cup.

To say he put on an impressive show is a gross understatement. You have to watch him to believe it. He gives his team the opportunity to attack by adding one extra defensive player to the side – him.

In a game against Chelsea in the UEFA Super Cup, Neuer made an assist to one of his teammates from Chelsea's own half.

That was something a defender or a midfielder should do. It's not something that comes with the job description of a goalkeeper; at least it never used to be. Once you get to see Neuer play in a few games, you will then understand why clubs are willing to pay so much money for him.

# Sergio Ramos – The 10th Champions League

In the 2014 UEFA Champions league, Real Madrid had a big problem to contend with before the final game. Their main and most talented defensive midfielder, Xavi Alonso, was unable to play. It was because Alonso had reached his maximum limit of yellow cards in the semifinal.

Because of this, Real Madrid's coach at that time, Carlo Ancelotti, had a real dilemma on his hands. Let's look at his options. He could choose using one of Alonso's substitutes, which seems logical. Then again, he could find his team a different, extraordinary solution. So what did he do?

Well, he didn't give the DM role to one of the team's other midfielders as you might expect. Instead, Ancelotti chose to put his right back player, Sergio Ramos, in the stopper role while keeping his main CB, Pepe, on the bench.

In this reshuffle, Ancelotti was also forced to use his German DM; Sami Khedira. Khedira had actually spent the last six months recovering from an injury. So how did things pan out? Fortunately for Ancelotti, his reshuffle turned out to be the perfect decision. Ramos stepped up to the challenge and played one of the best games of his life. Thanks to his ability to adapt, Madrid then went on to win their 10th Champions League title.

You might be wondering why Ancelotti chose to do things like this. It was quite simple actually. Ancelotti realized that he needed someone who could support Sami Khedira in the middle. This was important any time both Luka Modric and Angel Di Maria went to attack.

This would leave Khedira behind to secure the middle area. So Ancelotti had to have someone there who could play both as a DM and CB, and Pepe couldn't do that.

That's why Ancelotti kept him on the bench. Thanks to the smart thinking of Ancelotti, his incredible rearrangement turned out to be the right decision. It enabled his team to win the game by 4–1 and therefore his 10th Champions league title.

By the way, Ramos was the game savior. He scored a header in the 94th minute to tie the game. This sent the game into extra time where his teammates managed to score the three other goals.

# David Alaba

Austrian David Alaba (defender/midfielder) is another good example of an over qualified player. He plays for the Austria national team and the German side, Bayern Munich.

Besides being one of the best free kick takers in Europe, and perhaps the world, Alaba can also adapt his game with incredible skill. He can fit into many differing roles on the field. He can play as a center back, a defensive midfielder, and as a box-to-box player, but that's not all he can do.

Alaba can even play well on both sides, as a left or a right back. You can see now how beneficial it can be when you can use both of your feet with equal efficiency.

Alaba is not only able to send great crosses using any of his feet, but he can do it with high accuracy and with impressive power too.

His coaches at Bayern Munich, Jupp Heynckes and Pep Guardiola, depend on him because of his versatility. It's easy to see how a player's value can go up when he is able to adapt in this way.

Last year, Bayern Munich was asked if they would sell Alaba. One of FC Bayern`s executives, Karl-Heinz Rummenigge, said no way. In fact, he said they would rather sell their entire coaching staff and executive team before letting Alaba go. At just 23 years of age, Alaba has certainly got himself noticed.

You might be thinking there's enough to learn just by getting good at one position on the field. And you'd be right, that alone is a lot of work. And being good at one role is still enough to secure a lot of young players positions in professional soccer.

But if you want to excel and become more valuable and indispensable than the others, then you need more. Let's take a look at how you might go about achieving that.

First of all, you have to want to become complete. This is not something you should feel obliged to do, or do begrudgingly. You have to want it, and want it bad. Getting hungry and passionate about this is half the battle.

So you have to think BIG, and sometimes outside the box. If you thought you were already ambitious, you now need to take that ambition up to a whole new level.

This won't be difficult if you have the passion, the desire, and the determination to stand out. You will need to identify and improve every single weak point you have.

If any part of your game goes untrained, you won't flourish as a modern, complete midfielder. It's not so much the physical side that's challenging as your mental approach.

From the physical angle, you may find all skills easy to master. But if your mind doubts your ability, even if only a little, you won't ever cut the mustard. In short, if your mind is on side, then your body will follow. It won't work the other way around though.

OK, if you've got the right mindset, it's time to honestly look at your game. See what you're good at and what you're not. Your goal here is to become great at what you're bad or average at.

For any existing skills that you think you're good at, you have to aim now to make them extraordinary. Never settle for anything less. Don't try to be as good as someone else, strive to be even better.

Let's say you're good at reading tactics and plays, as an example. In this case, do what Pep Guardiola did when he made himself a master at reading other team's passes and playing styles. Zoom in and use the same obsessive approach for working with any other skills that need developing.

Look at them all, speed, passing, shooting and so on. Once you identify what areas need work, you should then ask yourself what it is you lack "exactly," and how can you get it. To do this, look for the answers to this question:

*Now, and with my current skills, what can I offer to my team that is better and more unique than the rest of my teammates?*

Maybe you have a strong foot or good shooting skills. Whatever you're good at, there's always room for still more improvements. Improving your shooting skills could bring many benefits.

For instance, you may get better at fouls and shooting from outside the penalty area. You may need to enhance your headers so you can offer help when needed on aerial plays. Perhaps you could improve your passing skills.

This might help you to create decent counter attacks or in-depth passes. Anything you can do to help penetrate through your opponent's defensive line will prove invaluable. Whatever it is, if your skill is poor, make it better, and if it's good, make it exceptional.

Finally, try to play in all midfield positions for a decent amount of time. You're still young and that means you have time on your side. So every once in a while, try to switch positions with any of your teammates.

Ask your coach to test you in different positions, even if they are different from your main role on the field. Try to play as a winger when your main role on the field is defensive midfielder, as one example.

Why should you do all this? Well, the more you try, the sooner you get to discover everything there is to know. You will learn about your true abilities and your inabilities.

You will most likely find some surprises along the way too, and good ones at that. Many of us have hidden talents; in all kinds things, not only soccer.

Yet most people never get to discover their latent talents. This is because they never get an opportunity to try at something they might be good at. In the soccer sense, the more you try the better it is.

Focus especially on the stuff that's outside your usual comfort zone. By doing this, you are more likely to uncover more surprises.

improve:
(1) what you're good at to become great.
(2) what you're poor at to become good.
(3) identifying weaknesses.
(4) mental side.

# 15. You Play Only with One Foot

Being able to play with your left and right foot is a real asset to you and your team. If you can play with them both, and with the same accuracy and the same strength, then it's even better. This ability is one of the most important features that any complete soccer player can possess.

Using both legs has so many advantages. To start with, it enables you to play on both flanks, as a right or a left winger.

This is something you can use to give your team a real edge anytime you want to surprise the opponents. When you change positions from one side to the other, it can disrupt the flow of the rival side's playing style.

Another good thing about being able to use both legs is when taking shots at the goal. For wingers, this is important. The ability to shoot with either foot helps you anytime you want to go deeper inside the penalty area.

When you have the option to choose which foot to shoot with, you have a much better chance of scoring a goal or making an alternative pass.

Here's one of the moves that Arjen Robben is best known for. Robben's loves to run on the right side (he's a RW) before moving toward the middle of the penalty area.

From there, he smashes a strong ball at the opposite side of the goal. This is something the two-footed player does with impressive frequency.

Being able to use either foot also makes your crosses a lot more dangerous. The best of the best on the flanks are the wingers and full backs that can send a cross while they're still running. Think of that for a moment.

A player who is only able to shoot with one foot often has to waste time by switching feet before playing the cross. As you know, a couple of lost seconds in soccer can result in a lost ball or a lost opportunity.

Worth noting too are the curvy crosses. These are played using the same foot of the same side, that is, a cross played from the left side with the left foot, and vice versa.

These crosses are more effective and create more danger on the opponent's goal than those played with opposite feet.

Let me explain. Let's say your one and only dominant foot is your left one, and you find yourself playing on the right side. In these situations, most of your crosses will be useless.

Or if you do make the cross, they will be easy for the rival defenders to clear away. It's a different story though if you can play your crosses using your right foot in this case.

Finally, the ability to play using either foot will help you pass the ball anywhere on the field. When you have two feet at your disposal, you can create more spaces and more dangerous attacks.

Two-footed players can move the ball with more accuracy and speed to the opposite side. This is because they don't have to waste time fixing their positions so that they can receive the ball with their one and only dominant foot.

To be able to use both feet with equal effect means that both your feet are dominant.

A player can be good, or even exceptional with one foot. Even so, he is still at a disadvantage compared to any player who can use both his feet. All you have to do is look at the most successful and the most valuable strikers in soccer right now.

All these players are capable of using both left and right foot equally, and from any position. The advantages don't only apply to strikers, of course, but too all field players.

# How to Improve Your Non-dominant Foot

*[handwritten: (1) Passes using all parts of foot +] (2) Work on accuracy. (3) Work on power.*

*[handwritten in margin: احبك ! بسو (smiley)]*

If you have never attempted to play with your weak foot before, prepare for a little frustration. If it feels like an impossible task at the start, just know that it will get easier, that's as long as you don't give up.

The most important thing here is to start slow and be patient. It will be an awkward feeling at first, so you have to ease things in until the weak foot gets used to the ball.

The best way forward is to start with some easy exercises. This will include things like simple passing drills. You will also want to kick a ball against a wall and then receive it with the same weak foot.

Once you get used to the ball you can move the practice up a notch. When you're ready, work at flipping the ball and do some back heel kicks. As you practice these drills, be sure to use both the inside and outside of your weaker foot.

Once you start to get comfortable using the ball with your weaker foot, it's time to start work on accuracy.

## Focus on Accuracy

It's best to start on accuracy using some foul sticks. *[handwritten checkmark]* What you do is place them at different locations on the field.

Your aim is to then kick the ball at the sticks from different angles and various positions. Your goal here is to enhance the accuracy or sensitivity of your weaker leg.

Don't expect miracles at the start. The accuracy phase will also feel awkward to begin with. It doesn't matter if your balls come out weak or inferior compared to those you send with your dominant foot.

In fact, you should expect this at the start of your accuracy training. Remember, patience and persistence is what always prevails in the end.

## Work on Power

By the time you get to this stage, you should be much more comfortable using your weaker foot. You will also have some degree of accuracy. Now it's time to look at strengthening both the weaker foot and its leg.

You can begin by taking different positions outside the penalty area. Work at both near and far positions. The idea here is to send fast, strong balls toward the upper and lower corners of the goal.

You will find this to be the toughest exercise of them all. Even if your accuracy is quite developed by now, it will be of no use to you until you can pack a strong kick.

Again, don't give up or lose hope. Even if it feels like an impossible task, I can guarantee that you will get better at it the more you practice. It might not feel like that at the time, but you WILL get there sooner or later, winners always do.

This stage may take you a month or more of continuous practice before it starts to feel more natural. As you become better at it, you can then work on playing backwards.

You can even practice bicycle-kicks if you feel confident enough. By this stage, you will be feeling pretty good about yourself.

Remember to never give up just because it's tough. The more obstacles you can get over as you develop your game, the better you will become.

Best of all is that each new challenge will get that much easier the more you develop your playing style.

# 16. You Don`t Position Yourself Well

The former Dutch professional player and now manager, Johan Cruyff, has a special way of looking at soccer. He also has a distinctive way of talking about the game. Here's a how he defines a great player, and I quote:

*"When you play a match, it is statistically proven that players actually have the ball three minutes on average … so, the most important thing is: what do you do during those 87 minutes when you do not have the ball. That is what determines whether you're a good player or not."*

The way a midfielder positions himself on the field is the one thing that can either make or break him. Your success at fulfilling your duties will depend on two main positioning strategies.

It also depends how you read the game before and after you take your position. We will look at each of these positioning strategies in turn.

## The Space Between Defense and Attack

*Either close to a player whom the ball is going to or between him and the passer.*

You will need to pick the best place to close gaps between the defensive and the attacking line of your team.

Always ask yourself where the next pass will likely head to. Once you find a suitable answer, place ①yourself in a position that allows you to intercept the ball. To do this you need to position yourself close to the next player who you think will receive the ball.

②An alternative is to be at an equal distance from the passer and the player waiting for the ball.

From this position you should be able to block the ball quite easy. That's if you're playing in the defensive midfield of course.

## Position Yourself Where You Can See Everything

The more players you can see, the more passing angles you will have to choose from.

*Learned this from Isaac, a colleague of mine.*

Put another way, the better your view is of the field, the more effective you become in the midfield. Make sure you stay in a continuous state of motion. This is better than settling down or standing still.

You need to always be looking to create space so that the other players can send you the ball if they need to. You also need enough space around you so that you can play the ball without too much pressure from the nearby opponents.

Before you act in any situation you need to ask yourself the questions below. Don't worry about the number of questions.

It takes you a lot longer to read them than it does to run the various scenarios around in your head. This is something that will come natural to you, and in nanoseconds too, once you are aware of your options.

- What are the potential shooting/passing angles available to me?
- How can I contain the ball holder and cover as many angles as possible?
- What are all the passing options available to the ball holder?
- How should I position myself so that I'm able to catch the next pass or cross before it reaches the man I'm marking?
- Should I open up the play and move the ball to the other side?
- When should I stick to my position and when should I leave it?
- When should I interfere with the play and how?

- Where am I from the penalty area and where am I from my teammates (especially the nearest one of them)? How can I clear more space for them or assist so that I can get them in front of the goal?
- What's the next possible scenario for the ball holder to follow?
✓ - What action should I take if the ball holder gets past me (a very important question for any defensive midfielder to ask)?

When you know how to position yourself well, you then get to make a huge difference to the way you perform. Good positioning creates better options and better options mean better outcomes.

Get better at:

(1) Knowing when to interfere and how.

(2) Covering as many possible shots and passes as possible.

(3) What to do when someone gets past you.

# 17. Not Having Good Shooting Skills

There's a retired Brazilian player called Roberto Carlos that you may know of. If you've never heard of the man, don't worry. His name is not so important here. What we want to focus on is his soccer legacy.

Carlos is perhaps the best left back to have played soccer in the last 25 years or more. He actually set a new standard for how a left and right back should play their game; a standard that has been in place ever since.

The whole reason of having a left or right back on the field was to stay tight and wait for the attack. That's before Carlos came along and changed it all.

To understand this better, we have to go back in time a bit. We're going to a time when the Catenaccio Italiano tactical system was in place (Catenaccio Italiano means the Italian chain, in English).

This system was most famous in the 1980s and 90s. It was, to all intents and purposes, a tactical system with a strong emphasis on defense. It was a strategy, and one that teams used often to help organize their defensive lines better.

The main idea of this system was to defuse attacks from the opposition and play on counter attacks or set pieces. But Carlos wasn't just a good solid left-back; he was the attacking solution that every team dreamed of.

Carlos wasn't just fast either; he was the fastest player in the world. It was a position he held for an entire decade.

He was so good with crosses that he managed to score goals from corner kicks and other dead spots close to the corner. The most important skill that Carlos had was his lethal left foot.

His contribution as a left back was invaluable. Besides that, Roberto Carlos was also great at scoring goals from free kicks. This was especially the case with free kicks played from far away.

Carlos was second only to Brazilian midfielder, Antônio Augusto Ribeiro Reis Jr, or just Juninho to his fans. Juninho was famous for his bending free kicks.

He was so good at them that many would say he was the greatest free-kick specialist of all time. As for Carlos, he had a familiar style, one that his rival players feared.

He would pace 15-20 feet behind the ball, pause, and then perform a quick run. As he reached the ball he would blast it toward the opponent's goal with incredible force.

So how powerful were his free kicks?

Put it this way. Standing in the wall against Roberto Carlos was a nightmare for every defensive player. Some of his goals came about because the players standing in the free kick wall moved out of the way. I'm serious.

They were worried about their safety so much that they would dodge his ball rather than feel the brunt of it. It's true. They would sooner let one of his balls pass rather than try to prevent it from reaching the goal.

You have to see it to believe it. They would sometimes step aside to avoid a whack from Carlos' flying missiles.

Roberto Carlos was incredible when it came to scoring from fouls. Many fans would agree that Carlos took the best free kick in the history of soccer. It was in a competition against France, in an exhibition game.

The free kick was 30 yards away from France's goal. Carlos moved back to the edge of the circle of the center line.

He then took his usual long run at the ball and miraculously swung it with his left leg at a top speed of 105 mph. France's goalkeeper, Fabien Barthez, had no chance.

All Barthez could do was stand by and watch as the ball smashed into his net. You should be able to find the clip on YouTube. Just search for: Best free kick ever by Roberto Carlos 1997.

120

If you're to excel, you must understand how important your shooting skill is. Strong accurate shots are fundamental to the success of any great midfielder. This is not something you need to be good at. It is something you must become exceptional at.

In fact, you should strive to be as good as a real striker. To build your shooting skills requires you to improve in two areas. The first is your shooting (1) accuracy and the second is your shooting power. Let's look at each of these in turn. (2)

## Shooting Accuracy

You rarely see a professional soccer player send a shot that misses its target by more than 10 or 20 yup. inches. Sometimes a shot will miss the mark by a considerable amount, but not that often, not with the pros.

Strong winds, or wet and slippery conditions can sometimes see wild balls. But under more normal conditions, good players are consistent with their accurate shooting.

A good midfielder has a good sense of where their target is and they know how and where they have to send their next ball. Whatever other skills a player might have, if his shooting falls short, then so will he.

This is why it's so important that you develop this skill. You want to get to the point where you're confident of reaching your target more often than not.

Good accuracy and follow-through technique is essential for all ball sports, not only soccer. Do a quick search on YouTube for David Beckham and Roger Federer.

Note how both these guys work miracles using their shooting skills. One uses his foot, the other his hand. Both are impressive and both have accuracy.

The only way you can expect to excel with your shooting accuracy is with practice. Repetition is the key here.

You must work at your shots day after day, whenever you get the opportunity. This is one drill that most soccer players don't mind doing.

The love affair between a player's foot and the ball is as addictive as an angler's hand and his fishing line. So spend plenty of time training and even spend whole nights on the training ground if you want to. The secret here is diversity. You need to practice sending your balls from every single position on the field.

You will want to create solutions for both yourself and your team whenever you feel stuck. The only way to do this is to have full confidence in your shooting ability.

There will always be occasions when you see a scoring opportunity as the best option to you at that time. The only way to take advantage of such situations is if you have a good, accurate shot. OK, let's look at how best to work on this skill.

When you practice, choose the most unusual, the most awkward places on the field to shoot from. This means the toughest angles and the widest positions.

*I do that! do more.*
*good job Abe.*

Practice shooting from these places, and keep at it until you become real good. Include low balls, high balls, direct kicks, free kicks and more. Your shooting opportunities will sometimes be unpredictable, and awkward.

This is why you need to have confidence shooting from anywhere at any time, and from any angle. So as you practice, don't leave any place on the field where you haven't gotten comfortable shooting from. This is especially important in and around your own domain.

To give you an example of how important this is, let's look at a competition between Barcelona and A.S. Roma.

This was a game in the Champions league where things weren't going too well for the Italians. They were having a real tough time reaching Barcelona's penalty area.

Despite playing in Rome, the Roma side just could not seem to get their act together. Then, to the surprise of everyone, the Italian team managed to score against Barcelona. So how did that come about?

Well, the goal came from an impressive shot by the Italian right back, Alessandro Florenzi. He sent a strong ball from a few meters above the center line, about 45-50 yards.

The ball went over the keeper's head and landed neatly in the goal. This is the kind of thing you have to be able to do if you're to become a valuable midfielder.

You must add value to your team whenever they need it. This is why you have to practice and practice a lot. In the case above, Florenzi was able to produce a "rabbit out of the hat" moment, just when his team needed it.

Remember, knowing how to shoot is not the same as being able to shoot. The latter can only come about with lots of relentless practice. Whatever you read, or whatever advice someone gives you, none of it is any good until you take action.

As with learning any skill, don't get put off or frustrated if things don't go too well at first. All you have to do is tell yourself that it's quite normal to struggle a bit when trying to develop a skill.

Occasional setbacks are normal, but they are also great to learn from. They show you what not to do, and that's valuable. The guys who become great are those who push forward no matter what stumbling blocks come their way.

In short, you will learn more from your failed attempts than you will from your successful ones. So look at failed attempts as your friend. Learn from them, don't curse them, or beat yourself up because of them. This is important.

Here's something worth noting: Your shooting accuracy is proportional to the number of shots you practice. When you practice a lot of shots, your accuracy and style will begin to develop naturally.

## The: 200 x 30 Routine

Here is one exercise that you will want to perform daily. I suggest you do it either in the morning or before bedtime. Your task is to practice 300-500 shots at the goal from different angles and places on the field.

124

*(1) work on abs.*
*(2) one-leg lunges.*

Do this for 30 consecutive days. Don't skip a day or take a Sunday off either. Continuity is the key here. After 30 days you will marvel at just how much your performance has improved in a single month.

Here are five steps to follow to make your shots more powerful.

1. Tighten your core (abs). This is so that you can make sure you're transmitting enough power from your body to the ball. It's like collecting energy before an explosion.

2. Make sure you have free movement with your foot (the one that is to strike the ball). Again, this is so that you have enough energy to kick the ball hard.

3. Perform explosive one leg lunges *?*

## How to Perform One-leg Lunges

Begin by taking the one leg lunge position. All this requires is to place one leg forward with the knee bent. Keep the foot flat on the ground. The other leg is behind you. *exer-cise.*

OK, when you come up, start kicking with your knee as if you're actually trying to strike someone with it. This exercise will increase the explosiveness from your knees. It will help you to launch a fast kick with plenty of power. This is useful when a fast approaching opponent is putting pressure on you.

4. Run before you kick the ball

(3) run before kicking the ball? I kn 😊

(4) learn from the masters ✓.

This is something that will depend on the place you receive the ball. It will also depend on the number of players around at the moment of shooting. There is, however, a general rule here, and that is:

Whenever possible, try to run before kicking the ball if it's an option. This will provide you with extra power when you strike the ball. It will mean you have a better chance of reaching your target.

## 5. Learn from the masters

There is no better way to learn than from the masters. In your case, I encourage you to search video footage of two players. One is the Swedish forward, Zlatan Ibrahimovich.

The other is a Brazilian winger/forward, called Hulk. And yes, there is a player called Hulk. These two are the most powerful shooters in soccer right now. Both guys are well-built and brutal with their shots.

They are very well-known in the soccer world to the extent that they create fear wherever they go. Those who fear them the most are goalkeepers and defenders. If you faced any of them, you would understand why this is.

Another great master is Hakan Calhanoglu, who plays for Turkey and Bayer Leverkusen. Calhanoglu. He is one of the best free kick takers in Europe right now.

Not only that, but he's also the best long-distance free kick taker in the world. When he used to play for Hamburg, he once scored a wonderful goal against Borussia Dortmund.

This was from a free kick a few meters above the center line. You might want to search for that on YouTube. For Calhanoglu, a free kick is like a penalty. He's so good at them that defenders panic whenever he gets a free kick against their side.

Watch the way the defenders of F.C. Köln looked *[rl.* before he scored a goal against them and you'll realize how good he is at taking fouls from any distance on the field. *watch it-*

---

## Learn to Shoot with Accuracy on the First Shot

As you play soccer you will sometimes receive unexpected balls. These will be the ones that rebound from the ground or deflect from other players and end up at your feet. You need to practice so that you are prepared in these situations.

Watch goals scored by Steven Gerard with Liverpool and Patrick Vieira with Arsenal. Here you will get to see firsthand the skill of great box-to-box players, and see how they deal with unexpected balls.

# 18. Not Mastering Crosses and Long Passes

Whatever position you take on the field there is one thing you will always need to know how to do. That is, send quality crosses to your teammates. This is especially important if you play wide on the wings.

When sending crosses you should not just kick the ball so that it reaches your attacking teammate. Your emphasis needs to always be on accuracy. That means you have to aim your crosses to reach him in a way that makes it easier for him to score. *Same for other positions!*

It might be better if he uses his head rather than his foot, or vice versa. Reading the situation will help you to make the best informed decision at the time.

Your job is to send a cross that makes it easy for your teammate, but hard for other team's keeper and defensive players. In short, your crosses should be accurate, quick and dangerous.

OK, before we move on with how you should practice, let's first take a look at these qualities in a real player. For this example I will use the English soccer star, David Beckham to illustrate the points. Beckham is perhaps the best set piece takers of the last 20 years.

## About David Beckham

Beckham has won the triple Premier league, The Champions League, and The FA Cup. He did all at his beloved Manchester United, before joining Real Madrid in 2003. At Real Madrid he became part of their dream team – The Galácticos.

This was the most expensive soccer team ever put together. It included players like Zinedine Zidane, Luis Figo, David Beckham and Ronaldo (the Brazilian).

David Beckham, who retired from soccer in 2013, was by far the best ever player at crosses and curvy fouls.

In one game, in the Spanish league against Deportivo La Coruna, Beckham made one of the best crosses I have seen. Another memorable event was when Beckham assisted Ronaldo to score.

On this occasion it was from a wonderful curvy cross that he played from a dead angle, near the center line. Beckham is the only player to have a movie named after him. You might be familiar with the title; "Bend it Like Beckham."

I recommend that you spend time watching videos for Beckham. Study the way he plays and try to mimic his crossing style. He was a real genius, that's for sure. You can certainly learn a lot from one of soccer's greatest ever celebrities.

OK, let's now take a look at the rules for playing great crosses. Here we will start with accuracy.

## Accuracy

Ideally, your cross should be easy for your teammate to translate into a goal or a dangerous chance. This means your cross should never go behind your teammate. If it does, he may well miss it.

Another thing to be aware of is not to pass the ball to your teammate direct. If you do that, he won't have an immediate opportunity to take a run at the ball and get that extra power behind his shot. Being able to perform a small run or stretch can make a big difference in these situations.

Accuracy is not just about reaching your target. It's also about making an accurate pass. To do this, always be mindful that your teammate should go and meet the cross rather than receive it direct.

# Force the Keeper to Stay in His Position

If your teammate is not waiting for your cross on the near post, you must keep all crosses - played from either side - away from the goal area. This will force the keeper to stick to his goal instead of going after the ball.

You don't want him chasing the ball in these situations as it will only add extra pressure on the teammate who's to receive it.

Your pass should also be fast, and the faster the better. This way, the goalkeeper doesn't have too much time to prepare himself for saving the ball.

A fast cross may also tempt the keeper to leave his goal and go after the ball. If he does that, and it's a real fast ball, he might just miss it. That will leave his goal empty for your teammate to place his header into.

To recap: The most effective cross is fast and curvy (back-spinning). And it should be between the six-yard line and the penalty kick sign.

# The One Second Acceleration

The quality of the cross depends on the quality of your run. And the quality of your run depends on the speed at which you can perform it. This is an important skill that will help you a lot when dealing with aggressive defenders.

It's useful in particular when faced with those who are strong, heavy and a bit slow. Your take off speed is what I call the one-second acceleration.

When dealing with strong defenders you need to escape fast. I'm not only referring to your running speed here, but also your ability to accelerate real quickly.

So what does it mean to have good acceleration? It means you get to move from the stand-still position to your fastest sprint in the blink of an eye.

This is the only way you will escape any tough defenders who are marking you. A quick take off also gives you the momentum needed to apply the power necessary for a strong shot. As you know, the more power you can apply to your cross, the faster and more dangerous it becomes.

The one second acceleration is just another skill. And like all skills, once you have developed it, you need to maintain it.

There are exercises and techniques that can help you work on this essential skill. Explosive leg exercises, like frog jumps and box jumps, can help a lot.

If you have the chance, see if you can train alongside other sprinters. You will get a lot of inspiration from these guys if you can. It will certainly encourage you to push your limits like nothing else can.

# Avoid Sending Low Crosses When...

There are only certain times when you should play crosses low to the ground or along the ground. These are in counter attacks where there are very few defenders around to clear the ball away.

When playing a low cross, the emptier the penalty area and the closer you are to it, the better. This makes the low cross more dangerous to the rival side. Avoid low crosses in all other situations whenever you can.

# Keep Your Low Cross Diagonal

Always do whatever you can to keep a low cross away from the goalkeeper. It's better to play them from angles rather than straight at the goal line or inside the goal area. Never give the goalkeeper the chance to come out of his goal to intercept your low crosses.

The most effective low crosses are those you send to your attackers coming from behind. Rival defenders won't be aware of them and the goalkeeper will have no chance to come out for the ball.

# Practice Targeted Long Passes to Anywhere on the Field

There will be times when you will have to send long passes to create counter attacks. Such situations are most likely to occur when you receive the ball after a corner against your team.

I have outlined some useful exercises below that will help you master long passes. Follow these and you will soon be able to send long, accurate passes to your attacking teammates.

If you have them, grab one of those wooden frames that teams often use for setting the wall before playing fouls. If not, get something else that is visible from a distance. This is to substitute a teammate.

OK, you need to place your wooden frame, or other visible object, at the far end of the field. Now return to the pile of soccer balls and practice kicking them hard and direct toward the frame. Your aim here is to have the ball land just a few inches from the distant object.

Repeat this drill about 100 times. Don't move the frame to a new position until you complete at least 5-10 successful passes. If that means repeating the exercise a few times over the course of a few days, then so be it.

When you've achieved your objective, it's time to move on to step two. This time, place another wooden frame, or other visible object, at the other side of the field.

What you're doing here is increasing your options. It means you have to decide which way to play the ball for the counter attack. Be spontaneous with your decisions.

OK, after completing step two, try to then play long passes using your weak foot. This will give you a variety of options to choose from. If you get good at using your weaker foot you get to send even more dangerous passes.

# 19. Not Scoring from Corners and Air Plays

Earlier in the book we looked at the explosive jump. We saw how you can develop and maintain this jump to best effect. Below are four rules that, when followed, will help you to score headers more easily using the explosive jump.

There is no doubt that mastering these skills will give you a definite edge over other players. Having the ability to handle crosses, high through balls and set pieces will get you noticed too.

Once you get good at these kinds of things, your role in the team becomes ever more valuable. With these abilities, you can add new tactics and new plays into your game style, and that's a powerful thing.

OK, let's look at these four rules in some detail.

# 1. Take a few steps to the front.

It's important that you take a few steps toward the ball instead of waiting for it to come to you. To begin with, you have a better chance to reach the ball before any of your opponents do.

Taking a short run up to the ball also allows you to create extra energy. You need this to generate enough power to get a good strike on ball with your head. Remember to always run at the ball from a diagonal angle in the penalty area.

# 2. Use your forehead when shooting in the same direction as your movement.

Whenever you need to send the ball in the same direction as your run, always use your forehead to strike it. This approach is a lot more effective than using the sides of your head. Try your best to keep the ball in a straight line, and direct it at a slight upwards direction.

What this does is allow you to send a strong ball at a lethal height (mid-range and above). A successful header like this is quite difficult for the keeper to save. The faster and higher your header shot is, the more difficult it becomes for the keeper to catch or deflect.

# 3. Lean forward when playing a side header.

You approach your headers in a different way whenever you want to send the ball in a different direction to your run.

In this case you need to lean forward and use the side of your head to strike the ball toward the direction you want.

When you head the ball at an angle like this, it's far more effective than a strong kick with the foot. And if you can, combine the shot with both speed and direction.

This will obviously make it even more dangerous. The important thing to keep in mind here is to avoid directing the ball toward your shoulders or hands. That might sound easy but believe me, this happens a lot.

# 4. If you can't play the ball at an angle, bounce it off the ground.

Sometimes the goalkeeper will be in a good position to save or deflect your shot and you know it. In situations like these it's better that you try a different approach. If you can try to send him a bouncy header, instead of the more direct shot that you might have planned to do.

Why do this? Well, when you head the ball at the ground it changes direction, and with any luck that will confuse the goalie. What you mustn't do is just head the ball to the ground and hope for the best.

The secret behind a successful bouncy header is to aim the ball at the middle ground. That is, the space between you and the goalmouth, or close to it. Let me explain why.

If you bounce the ball on the ground too close to yourself, it will lose power. When that happens, it won't reach enough height to beat the goalie. If you bounce the ball too close to the goal line, it will have enough power but it's too late.

In this situation, the ball won't go high enough to make it a difficult save. This is why you aim for the middle ground every time; somewhere between you and the goal line.

# 20. Not Knowing How to Take a Penalty

The best penalty taker in England is a defender named Leighton Baines. He is 30 years old, has been playing for Everton for the past eight years. Baines' is the second best scoring defender in England, right after John Terry.

He's also the number one penalty taker in the English international team. He even comes before Wayne Rooney on the penalty taking list of England's greatest.

So how good is he? Well, Baines has only ever missed one penalty in his 10 years of playing domestic championships. Those tournaments include the English League, the FA Cup, and the League Cup.

The one and only missed penalty happened in 2015, in a game against Manchester United. It was United's goalkeeper, David de Gea, who managed to save Baines' late penalty. This was much to the surprise of many, given Baines' record up until then.

Every soccer fan knows about Baines. He's even famous as a penalty-taking superstar in the virtual world too. What am I talking about? The online *Fantasy Premier League game, that's what. I'm sure you've heard of that. Those who take part in this game choose Baines to take their penalties more than any other player. If you follow English soccer you will know of his excellent reputation. It's not just penalties he's famous for either. Baines is also a force to be reckoned with when it comes to taking free kicks too.

*The "Fantasy Premier League game" is the official online Fantasy Football game of the Premier League. It has over three million players at the time of writing. In fact, Fantasy Premier League is the biggest Fantasy soccer game in the world right now, and best of all is that it's free to play. You can also win some great prizes if you get good. To get started, you pick your squad, create and join leagues and select your team each week.*

# When the Team's Captain Slips

Earlier in the book we looked at the English center back, John Terry, who plays and captains Chelsea. Terry has some great goal scoring skills yet oddly enough he isn't so good at penalties.

I will use an incident from 2008 to illustrate. This was a game where Chelsea met Manchester United in the UEFA Champions league final.

Terry was preparing to take the final penalty. On his run-up to the ball, he slipped just as he was to take the shot. This failed attempt was Chelsea's final opportunity to win. If Terry had succeeded, Chelsea would have won their first ever Champions league title.

This slip was devastating for the Chelsea side and their fans. I'm sure it was embarrassing as well, seeing the team captain blunder like that.

They had put a lot of faith in him, hoping he would help lead the team to victory in their first major trophy. Needless to say that this is one of those awful memories that every Chelsea fan would love to forget, but can't.

# How the Shootout Works

There are times in a penalty shootout where the teams fail to finish the game from the first five penalties. In cases like this, the shootout will continue on until the tenth or the eleventh penalty. You might have to take one of the penalties yourself, even if you're not good at it.

There's no escaping this. It's a written soccer rule that you just can't avoid. This is why you must have the skills necessary for good penalty shots, just in case. That means you have to practice shooting penalties just like any other team player.

It doesn't mean practicing only every now and again either, but on a regular basis. Remember, even if you get good at something, you can't hold on to it unless you maintain the skill. As you know by now, the only way to maintain a skill is through regular practice.

In general, a team captain will usually find himself on the list of the first five penalty shooters. Even if you're not the captain, and you don't know how to shoot a penalty, you may still find yourself on that list.

For this reason, you should always be ready, willing and able to take a penalty. Don't ever forget, soccer is a team sport, and your teammates need to know that they can rely on you. So if ever you get called upon to take a late penalty, let the guys have confidence in you as you approach the mark.

# How to Perfect Your Penalty Kick?

There are two essential attributes you need to be successful at penalties. The first is the right mindset and the second is the right method. Let's look at both of these in turn.

# The Right Mindset

Even if you play against an average goalkeeper, the way you think about him at the time will affect the way you shoot. If you think negative thoughts, then negative things will happen in reality. So if you doubt yourself or believe that you might miss the penalty, then you most likely will.

Let's see how you might get out of this situation, this negative mindset. You have two options here, visualization and technique.

# Visualization

The first is to change what you see. So instead of doom and gloom scenarios running through your mind, try to change your focus. Pessimism or despondency will deliver for you just fine, but deliver the wrong results. You have the power to consciously change this.

Focus on seeing the ball hit the goal net, that's all. And keep this image in your mind before and during the penalty. Believe me when I say this visualization approach can work like magic. But then again so can the reverse thinking, but in the wrong way. You choose.

# Block Outside Distractions

If you don't doubt your ability to score, but worry about nerves, then you can try a different approach. In this case you have to take your mind off the penalty as you wait for your turn.

Once again, it is conscious thinking that comes to the rescue here. Anytime you have the jitters, just try to focus on anything outside the game (see below). Continue to do this until your turn comes to take a penalty, then switch your focus back to the shot.

So before the penalty, focus on what you're going to have for dinner later, if that helps. Or maybe you're better off focusing on something physical.

In this case, read the banners behind the goal, focus on the fans, or even on the goalkeeper's shoes. It doesn't matter what it is as long as it works. Having something to distract you in the run up to your turn can be really effective, as long as you concentrate.

Basketball players actually work at blocking out distractions. There is this unusual approach they use when they practice free throws. What they do is have someone try to distract them with a whistle or a buzzer, or even a slight hit.

The idea is to become super-focused on the task at hand. In other words, you're oblivious to anything else that's going on around you. If you're prone to outside distractions, then you might want to give something like this a go too. Try it to block other players (especially Teammates), comments. They only d[...]

# Technique

There are three types of shots that have the highest probability of success. If you can master them all, you will have a definite edge over other players and the opponent's goalie.

It means you get to choose the right type of shot for the given situation. Being good at all three will definitely help you to maintain your confidence levels.

To learn how to do each of these three shots well, will need quite a bit of practice. Because of this, you might want to just focus on one or two and become adept at them. The first of these three shots is perhaps the hardest of them all. Let's take a look at how to perform it.

OK, for this technique to work you will have to keep your eyes fixed on the keeper's legs. That might sound a bit odd, but just bear with me here. So focus on his legs and then run toward the ball.

Then, just before you get to the ball, slow down a little before you strike it. The technique here is quick-slowdown-strike.

The reason for the slowdown is to see if the goalkeeper reveals the direction of his dive. This is something he will hopefully do the second you slow you pace.

The idea behind this is that he might not have anticipated your slowdown before making his move. Once he reveals which way he's going to dive, you then kick the ball hard toward the opposite side. Of course, this all happens in nanoseconds.

The most important thing to note here is to make sure you don't stop completely before you strike the ball. If you do, then there's a good chance the ref will disqualify any goal you score.

This is because stopping is against the soccer law. So again, you need to run, slow down, and then play the ball. And play it toward the opposite direction of the keeper's movement, but never stop.

2) The second technique is to bend your body while taking the starting position. If you do this with conviction you force the keeper to think you're going to place the ball either to his right or left.

Your plan is to then to kick the ball with force, at mid to high range, toward the center of the goal. Whatever you do, don't send the ball too low or along the ground.

If you do that, there is still a good chance the keeper's legs will be in the middle of the goal area. Needless to say, his legs alone could block a ball that is low to the ground. When you keep your penalty kick high, there is no risk of his legs getting in the way of your shot.

3) The third type of penalty that has a better chance of success is one that Cristiano Ronaldo prefers. With this shot you aim at the inside of the net, either to the left or the right side. As you do, make sure you kick the ball with plenty of power.

This kind of shot is hard, and I do mean hard, for the goalie to catch or deflect. As long as you have enough speed and accuracy on the ball, you have a great chance to score. Even a skilled keeper like Gianluigi Buffon, has little chance of saving a shot like this.

I suggest you master at least one, preferably two, of these three shooting techniques. This way, whenever your turn comes to take a penalty, you have a much better chance of scoring for your team.

You may wonder why I have not said anything about sending the ball up to the top right or left here. The reason for this is because it's a risky approach, and one that requires a lot of practice.

You have many other skills to work on besides penalty shots. For this reason, it's better to stick with the ones that take up less of your training time.

OK, so stick to any one or more of these three techniques. Practice them until you become good at scoring penalties. And once you have mastered them, remember to maintain the skill along with all others. Leave the risky shots, those aimed at the top corners, to the likes of Arturu Vidal.

He is one of the most successful penalty takers in European soccer right now. In fact, Vidal rarely takes a penalty kick that isn't aimed at the top corners of the goal. Most of his penalties are lethal and reach the net regardless of how good the keeper is.

# Watch and Learn from the Penalty Masters

There is no better way to learn penalty shots than to study the techniques of the masters. There are three in particular that I think you should take note of. I have already mentioned two of these before.

They are Leighton Baines and Arturu Vidal. I also urge you to look at the English legend and penalty master, Matt Le Tissier. He used to play for Southampton in the 1980s and 90s. Le Tissier spent 16 long years with that club. He was yet another of those complete players that I talk about in this book.

Le Tissier was also a wonderful passer. He had good vision and a great ability to read the game. When it came to taking penalties, I would say that Le Tissier had one of the best shooting techniques ever. Moreover, he was the best penalty taker in the history of the English Premier League.

Even 13 years after his retirement with the Saints (Southampton), Le Tissier still holds the highest penalty scoring ratio in the history of the premier league. In fact, he only has one wasted penalty out of the 26 he took between 1986 and 2002. Let's look at these.

Le Tissier has a penalty ratio of 96.15%. This is better than all the other premier league legends. That includes Thierry Henry (92 %), Alan Shearer (83.58 %) and Wayne Rooney (68.15 %). It's also better than Manchester United's wonderful trio; Roy Keane, Ryan Giggs and David Beckham.

Be sure to watch Le Tissier's video clips. Pay particular attention to his shooting style. Honestly, he was one of the best of his time.

He scores from both short and long distances, and with high accuracy and huge power. If you study his clips carefully you will get to learn a lot.

# 21. Not Having Good Ball Control

When you receive the ball, you must make sure that it doesn't stray too far. This is the ABC of becoming a successful soccer player for any position.

In many situations you will find yourself with limited space and surrounded by opponents. All you need to know about those guys is that they are ready to steal the ball from you at the first wrong move you make. It's crucial that the ball stays as close to your foot as possible.

That ball should become like a natural extension to your foot/feet. What I mean by that is once you have possession of the ball you should feel comfortable and in complete control. When you're ready to pass it on, there are five basic rules you need to follow.

# Rule 1: Direct the ball to where you want to take it.

You might want to send the ball into a new empty space, or direct it to a nearby teammate. It doesn't really matter where you want to send it. What matters is that you know what you want to do with that ball once you receive it.

The most important thing about receiving any pass is to stay confident and be prepared. When you are confident, and know your next move and, you get to surprise the player marking you.

Don't forget, he can only guess (try to read) what you're about to do next. Only you will know for sure what that move will be.

# Rule 2: Always move toward the ball.

This is important and something that used to be one of my drawbacks. That was until I got to study my playing style on video, after which I corrected my whole approach. If you currently wait for a pass to reach you, that has to change, starting today. From now on, move toward the ball whenever possible.

In other words, go to meet the ball, and don't wait for it to arrive at your feet. You need to do this so that you can prevent the opponent next to you from intercepting the pass before it gets to you. Meeting the ball also gives you more space to escape your opponents.

## Rule 3: Always stay on your toes.

Don't put your weight on your heels as you receive the ball or while dribbling it. Being on your heels is never a good idea.

Why? Because resting on your heels will make you heavier. It interferes with your moves and the speed of your actions. The best approach is to stay on your toes whenever you're in possession of the ball.

## Rule 4: Use both feet.

I have written a full chapter on this point but I will go over it again here in brief. You have an incredible advantage when you develop the ability to use both your feet to equal effect.

This even applies to goalkeepers. Any two-footed member of a team is going to stand out above those who can only use their one dominant foot.

Moving the ball with ease, especially when dribbling, requires you to switch feet continuously. The better you can do this, the more successful you will be when it comes to getting past your opponents.

Look at all the professional players that you know of. You will see that the vast majority of them can play with both feet equally.

They become so good at it that it's hard to know which foot is their dominant one and which is, or was, their weaker foot.

You can be really good as a one-footed midfielder, there's no question of doubt about that. But if you want to shine above all others and become exceptional, then you will want to learn how to use both your feet.

## Rule 5: The ball should be close to you at all times.

Aim to occupy the smallest area possible when you play. Have that ball stick to you as if it were a part of your own foot. To do this, you have to have quick feet. That means you must practice moving with the ball anywhere and everywhere.

What you're doing here is getting to form a close relationship with the ball. There is nothing worse than the ball feeling loose and vulnerable at your feet. The more you two can attach yourself to the ball, the better you can perform.

Ronaldo de Assis Moreira, known to his fans as just Ronaldinho, is a Brazilian attacking midfielder or forward. He is the player who many consider to be the best ever when it comes to ball control.

He's even better than Messi and Maradona, both of whom are/were great in their ability to move and control the ball with incredible skill.

There will always be occasions when you're under attack on the field and find yourself in a real tight space.

Any player who can keep hold of the ball in these situations has a real talent. Ronaldinho, Maradona and Messi are perfect examples of this skill.

As for Ronaldinho, he said he began to develop this skill from early childhood. He used to take the ball everywhere he went.

In fact, he was never without a ball by his side. For you to become great at possessing and controlling the ball, you too need to keep one around you as much as possible. It becomes as much a part of you as an inanimate object can be.

Of course, when that ball comes into play it transforms into an animate object. Whenever your ball becomes active, both you and your brain connect with it. Some of this you do at the subconscious level, in much the same way as you connect with other parts of your body.

# The Square/Circle Drill

Draw a square or a small circle and stay in it with your ball. Spend as much time as you can, moving the ball anywhere and everywhere within the space. Neither you nor the ball must leave that circle, or at least that's your aim.

Keep doing this until you can spend long stretches inside the box without leaving it. The idea here is to get comfortable controlling the ball in a tight area.

When you become good at it; try to use smaller and faster balls. A tennis ball is a good start. If you think it's too difficult, don't! The German midfielder, Messut Ozil, plays with a ball of chewing gum in his pre-game warm.

So a tennis ball is huge in comparison. If you get good with a tennis ball, then you might want to move on to a golf ball. I can promise you this: If you can master smaller balls, once you switch back to a soccer ball, controlling it will then seem like child's play.

¹ Tried it and it worked with size 3 and 4 then switching to 5!

² update: Tried this with a tennis ball. I don't know if there's a difference but we'll see!

# 22. Not Being Familiar with the Other Team's Playing Style

A midfielder who does not study his opponents before a game will always remain at the amateur level. It's a common mistake and one which has negative consequences.

Those who do study their opponents, on the other hand, are at a much greater advantage than those who don't. In short, they get to play a much smarter, more successful game on the day.

*I dotted a lot.*

So how do you get familiar with the other team's players before a game? Well, there's the usual footage your coach makes you watch on video sessions before a game.

But these are often general. Yes, of course they are useful, but what I'm actually talking about here are the tiny details. These are the patterns of mistakes that your opponent's make.

These are the little things that you note about those players who will be marking you on the day in particular.

Many of these things will not always be obvious, not at a casual glance at least. This is why you have to look out for them. All players have their weak points as well as their strong points.

Getting to know what these are in your rival players puts you at a huge advantage. There will be parts of their game where they repeat the same or similar mistakes in certain situations. In a lot or cases, once you get to identify your opponent's points of weakness, you can then use it against them on the day.

Ideally, you need to read the attack, the pass and the through ball, as well as knowing who will move to where and when.

Knowing which opponents are going to play and how, puts you at an immediate advantage. By understanding your opponents, you are able to make much better informed decisions. Think about that for a minute.

Because you've studied the guys you're up against, you know how to defend and how to attack. This is a simple concept based on your newly acquired knowledge.

It also means you are in a better position to communicate and organize your teammates whenever necessary. This is especially useful for organizing your attack and defense lines.

Having the ability to read the game better also helps when positioning your teammates in set pieces. Defensively, if you're a DM or CM, you can do a much better job with organizing your defense in corners. You do this according to the things you have learned about the kick or the corner taker.

When you study their approach beforehand, it means you are better able to predict their actions. You will know things like how and where the corner taker will send his next corner or foul.

To read the game or the current play is a winning strategy. But it is most successful when done with study, more so than intuition alone. It helps you to position yourself and your teammates in the right place to clear the ball away.

Offensively, if you're the foul/corner taker or the team's playmaker, you need to switch your thinking. Now you have to know about the type of corners and crosses that works best on the rival team.

Again, if you have studied their players before the game, you will most likely know these things. You will know whether it's best to play a corner in the near post or when to keep it at the far post.

You will also know when to pass a corner or a foul and when and how to shoot. It will also pay you to know how the opponent's keeper reacts to long balls. For example, does he stick to his goal or does he come out after the ball? And if the latter, where does he deflect most of his clearances to?

Predicting the different scenarios of a game is a useful skill. And it's a skill that all successful midfielders acquire. Being familiar with the playing style of the opposite team is invaluable on game day, it really is.

Note how most teams and individual players rarely make dramatic changes to their playing style and game tactics. The majority of coaches, except for new coaches or the tactically flexible among them, tend to follow a set formula.

That is, they base their teams' tactics on the different strengths and weaknesses of their squad. Let's look at this a little closer.

Most British teams, except for a few among them, tend to play quite physical soccer. These are games that depend on high balls and crosses. These teams often choose their main striker based on his header skills.

For generations, this style of play has been rooted in English soccer and it rarely changes. Take a team like Stoke City, for example. They will play many crosses, which is a style of play that requires a special approach.

If you study how they play corners and set pieces, you soon become familiar with their style and their strategy. Any team that plays against Stoke City is up against at least five good players. They are strong, they are good at headers and they are above 1.88 m in height.

However, the defense of these teams is torn apart anytime they play against a side whose midfielders and attackers move the ball fast and along the ground.

# Ask Lots of Questions

It's always wise for you to ask yourself certain questions as you study soccer videos or live games. By doing this, you will find the answers you're looking for. Remember too, you are studying games and players here, you are not watching them.

You might get to find out quite a bit about your rivals so be sure to take notes as you go along. This is what I mean when I say study, as opposed to watch. When you study the game and its players, your mind is in a different mode.

OK, let's look at some of the questions you will want to prepare as you study the opposition.

- How good are they at rotating the ball, and how fast do they do it.
- Who's the fastest player and who's the slowest player?
- Who's the best attacker at air plays? Who's not so good at them? Who's not good at positioning? And who gets easily caught in the offside trap?
- Who's the best passer in this team? And where does he prefer to pass his balls to? How does he react when he gets exhausted?

Get to recognize the style of the other team's key player(s). See how they play through passes or send long balls. This knowledge will help you to anticipate a lot of otherwise dangerous balls early on. You will be able to react a lot faster too.

At the age of 36, the player Andrea Pirlo will send higher through-balls from wider areas. He does this instead of running. When you become aware of something like this, you can intercept long passes early on. That means you get to reach the ball long before any of your opponents do.

OK, back to the question list.

- Which player has the most agility and the highest fitness levels? Who gets exhausted early on that you can defeat with speed?
- Who is the most physically challenging player? Who is the least physically challenging?
- How good is the keeper with high balls, corners and crosses?
- How good is he in long shots? How are his diving skills?

Study the tendencies or the habits of your opponents from where they perform their plays. And for corners and set pieces, ask questions like:

- Where does the corner/foul taker prefer to send his balls and how?
- Does he send his corners too high or mid height?
- How fast does the opposition recover from their attacks? And how fast do they switch from attacking to defending, and vice versa?
- Who's the most skilled dribbler in the team?
- Are there any notable holes or gaps you can use to score goals?
- Is there any extra info you can pass on to your attacking players about the rival goalkeeper?

- How does the goalie deal with breakaways? Does he spread himself too quick or does he like to wait? Does he cover for long balls? How tall is he? And how can you use what you know about him to your own advantage?
- Are there any attacking patterns you can spot that they use to score?

What kind of questions you ask yourself will depend on what you want to know. You will at least want to include some of the above into your question list.

I'm sure you get the general idea though. Once you have your "questions template" I would suggest saving it as a file on your computer.

This way you can print out a new blank file for each team you prepare to play against. All you have to do then is fill in the blanks (answers). This is something that will undoubtedly give you an edge on game days.

Both your physical and your mental game are going to get a performance boost because of your pre-game prep. Remember to share your findings with your teammates. They should also study the teams themselves.

If they have done, then you will have a pretty powerful picture built up between you all. This means there's an excellent chance of your side dominating the game on the day of the competition.

# All Players Make Repeated Mistakes

After he had retired from soccer, the former Real Madrid legend, Roberto Carlos, confessed something in an interview. He said that he'd suffer whenever the guy he was watching on the left flank went deeper inside the field and switched roles with another teammate.

During his last days at Spain, he and his team had some bad games against Barcelona. This included a humiliating defeat in the Santiago Bernabéu Stadium that ended in 6-2. Real Madrid lost because of the continuous motion of the Barcelona players.

Barcelona had a smart strategy where their attacking line would often switch roles. Not only did they switch roles, but they did it fast too. This threw the Real players off every time.

So how do I know all this? It's because I studied the game in detail. Studying games and players is something you might want to get into the habit of doing too. It will put you in constant observation mode, which is a good thing.

It means you will get to pick up on a lot of stuff that other, less observant players miss. It's a great approach and one that will help you to master your game. You need to study your opponents completely. By doing this, you are much better able to use their weakest points against them. And that means you get to predict their offensive patterns and use them to improve your game strategy.

# 23. Not Being Familiar with the Defender You're Going to Mark – or the One Marking You

Let's assume you have finished your homework on the rival side. You should now be familiar with the tactics and playing styles of your opponents. OK, it's now time to move on to the next stage. You must now focus on studying your opponent's key players.

For you, it's important to focus on the main playmaker of the team if you're playing as a DM or CM. For reference, that's the opposite DM/CM if you're a playmaker/Regista. And it's the opposite LB/RB if you're playing as a winger.

For example, if you play on the defense side, you should be familiar with one important fact. That is, in any team there will be two or three key players. These are the dangerous guys, the ones who pose the greatest threat.

They are responsible for creating and scoring 80 percent of goals and goal-scoring opportunities. It goes without saying that these are the players you need to focus on most.

How to Study Key Players

To study these key players well, you have to look out for patterns. This includes any little tricks they might like to slip into their play every so often.

We all form habits, some good, others bad, and even the best of the best can't escape this. Bad habits can be hard to break though, impossible sometimes. This is especially true when the pressure is on.

High tempo, high pressure games are what see bad habits materialize. You see, there will be little things, quirks if you like, which are a part of who we are, no matter how hard we try to change.

Every single player, and I do mean all players, have something about their style that you can use to your advantage. Knowing what they are good at, as well as what they're not, all counts. That brings us on to how we can identify these patterns.

# Player Patterns

## Thierry Henry

Retired French forward, Thierry Henry, had a very unique style. He would stand in the offside for a little longer than usual, waiting patiently. He was waiting for any pass that a rival defender would send to his teammate.

When he did, Henry would charge in and try to snatch the ball and score a goal. If you want to see an example, then watch his goal against England in the 2004 European Cup.

Here Henry flipped the game upside down in the final minutes. What he did was intercept a pass from midfielder Steven Gerard to his keeper David James.

A while back I was watching some highlights for Manchester United's new French winger. His name is Anthony Martial. He's since earned himself a new nickname.

They call him "The New Henry." Why? Because he does the exact same thing that Henry used to do. He sneaks up behind a defender, waits for a wrong pass, and then steals the ball away at every opportunity.

# Filippo Inzaghi

Retired Italian striker, Filippo Inzaghi, is one of AC Milan's attacking legends. His nickname was "King of the Offside Trap." This is because he would fall for the offside five or ten times during a single game. He would do this until he got the opportunity to spring into action. His approach was simple yet effective.

He would wait until rival defenders felt safe. When the moment was desirable, he'd surprise them by making a quick move at just the right moment.

When successful, Inzaghi would find himself in a sudden one-to-one situation with their goalkeeper. They called him the King of the Offside Trap because he would often go on to score, thus making him a kingpin.

There's no doubt that Inzaghi was a goal scoring machine. Despite this, he wasn't talented, at least not in the usual sense. His mind was the only thing that made him one of the greatest strikers to ever play for Milan.

# Arjen Robben

Let's now look at the Dutch midfielder, Arjen Robben. Those of you who know him will be familiar with his selfish style. In fact, Robben's can be extremely selfish at times.

He is what we call a ball-hogger. He will only ever pass to his fellow teammates when it's necessary, and even that's no guarantee. He just loves to hold on to that ball for dear life once he gets possession of it.

There is a way to mark ball-hoggers like Robben. The best approach is to isolate them in the corner. You have to do this using a couple of players though.

This way you get to steal the ball from him without too much difficulty. It works because anytime they try to run with the ball, it's hard for them to keep it when there are two guys containing their moves.

As for Robben, there is another familiar style to the way he plays. He has a habit of running along the right flank. From there, he goes deeper into the field and then fires a strong shot toward the far post of the goal.

Like all ball-hoggers, he rarely crosses and he rarely passes. That's just part of who he is; it's his selfish style. He will try this trick whenever he finds the slightest opportunity to go for it.

Robben is not alone in this. You will come across many selfish players in your time. The best thing you can do is to familiarize yourself with them. As always, knowing how a player plays before a game gives you a much better chance of defeating him on the field.

From their repeated patterns you will know how and where they like to play their balls and shots. Once you can predict their moves, you get to position yourself so that you're prepared to respond.

The Arsenal winger, Theo Walcott, is another example of a ball-hogger. He won't pass the ball, not even if he's close to the goal and trapped in.

It's the same in a breakaway. He would sooner play a chip over the goalkeeper rather than do the sensible thing and pass the ball on to a better positioned player.

## Bacary Sagna

Now let's look at Bacary Sagna, the French right back. Sagna plays for the English club Manchester City, and the France national team.

When Sagna plays, he has a tendency to leave big spaces behind him whenever he moves to the front. Moving wide to play in these gaps will benefit any winger who plays against him.

In one game when playing with Arsenal against Borussia Dortmund, he went to support a corner. As he did this, he left more than 40 yards of empty space behind him.

Dortmund's attacker at that time, Robert Lewandowski, took advantage of this space and went on score a late goal for his team.

## Dennis Bergkamp

Dennis Bergkamp is a Netherlands's legend, but he had a strange approach to the way he played. He was one of those rare strikers who like to score from outside the penalty area. Bergkamp was the kind of attacker who would retreat to receive the ball from outside the penalty box.

Once he was in position, he would then send a strong shot or a lob over the goalkeeper's head. He was often successful too, which is why he did it of course. *had. (would have had ~).*

Again, anyone who knew the way Bergkamp liked to play would have an immediate advantage over him. Not that it would be easy because Bergkamp was a skilled player. But anyone who familiarized themselves *himself* with his style was in a much better position to defeat him on the field nonetheless.

Competing against him would force a defensive midfielder to meet him early in the penalty area. From there he could prevent leaving a space for Bergkamp to work his magic.

For the record, Bergkamp is one of the few attackers who have a similar number of assists as goals to his record.

To play against someone like Bergkamp is much easier for any team if the coach organizes his side right. If the coach is smart he will tell his DM to stick to the penalty box anytime that player holds the ball near to the area.

# The Conclusion

When you study player patterns you get to be more in control. There is nothing worse than running around a soccer field not knowing what to expect or when. *Exactly! I always say this to new players who either want to run or just to be physical. soccer is a smart game*

This won't happen when you're in control of your game. And to do that, you have to familiarize yourself with the rival team and its players. This is not an option, or some bolt-on skill, not if you're serious about becoming an exceptional player.

All great players take responsibility over everything that happens around them. This way they can leverage their performance and make it as perfect as possible. As Benjamin Franklin once said, and I quote:

"By failing to prepare, you are preparing to fail"

That single quote tells you everything you need to know. Failure is the inevitable consequence of not preparing before a game.

Study the players on the opposite team, especially the playmakers. Know how the play, know if there are recurring patterns in their game, and note their mistakes. Know what they're good at too. It's probably a recurrent pattern.

# 24. Not Playing on the Referee's Whistle

There is one common mistake that happens in almost every single game. It is a mistake that is especially typical for anyone who plays in defense. What happens is that the player suddenly stops playing the ball or marking an opponent. Why does he do this?

Because he thinks he deserves a foul and so he waits for the referee to give him what he wants. The problem is that the referee often doesn't respond.

That's bad news for the player who stopped playing because he's just taken himself out of the active game. The chances are that his actions, or in this case his inaction, have just put his team in grave danger.

The message here is a simple one, and that is to never assume anything. It doesn't matter how obvious something might appear to you.

It's what the referee sees, or doesn't see that's important in these situations. If the ref didn't see anything, or he didn't think the incident warranted a foul, then you're out of luck.

You certainly won't get to make his mind up for him in these matters. So here's what you need to do to save yourself the humiliation. It's actually a very simple solution too: Until you hear that whistle, keep playing on as normal.

If you don't heed this warning, then it will be to your detriment. This is even more important when the ball is inside the penalty area and you're calling for an offside or a regular free kick.

You can see the same thing happen in a fake offside. In this case, the defenders or the goalkeeper stops playing. Again, they just stand there and raise their hands, assuming the ref will award an indirect free kick. But he won't always do this. It then leaves the opponents with a golden opportunity to score a goal, without any distraction or resistance.

I have seen the same thing happen with forwards, wingers and playmakers. It occurs when they stop following the ball or moving toward the goal. They do this because they think they're in an offside position when they are not, or they are, but no official saw it.

This act of "stopping play" won't get you any benefits. If anything, it may cause you to lose a goal scoring opportunity. And even if you are in the offside, a linesman is only human after all. That means he can make mistakes, just like you, and not always see things he perhaps should have done.

No matter how tempting it might be to stop playing and wait for the referee to favor you with a foul, I say don't do it. Keep playing on every ball however much you think you're right in asking for the foul. Keep moving, and continue with the game, especially when the ball is inside the penalty area or close to it. This is always your best approach.

There will always be occasions when a lineman or referee feels hesitant to disallow a goal or call for an offside. They never make their decisions lightly, especially with borderline incidents.

They want to make sure they take the right action by making a fair decision. In borderline cases, they will look at you and see how you react toward a certain play. If you just keep playing as if nothing has happened, there's a good chance that the referee will keep the game going and call nothing on you.

I have already mentioned Philipo Inzaghi in this book. Some of the goals that Inzaghi has scored for A.C Milan were pure offside plays. Even so, he would always continue to play as if he was not in the offside position.

On many occasions, he would get to deceive the referee or the lineman by his attitude. Because of that, they would often give him the benefit of the doubt and allow him to continue playing. In these situations, Inzaghi would frequently go on to score.

*[handwritten margin note: lol?! really? :)]*

*[handwritten note at bottom: Conclusion: Stop complaining and always play on the whistle!]*

174

# 25. Not Having
## Confidence in Yourself

*I read it as "impressive ball skills" lol*

Confidence is more than just having a physical ability. What I mean by this is that it's no use being good at something if you are unable to use those skills when you need them most.

You may well be a decent height and have a strong, well-toned body. You might also have the ability to read the game and display some impressive ball skills.

And let's say you even make it into a half-decent team. You are, to all intents and purposes, a "good" player.

But here's the thing: being good does not make you great. It just means you are decent. And you will never be a great midfielder either, not if you don't believe in yourself and your abilities.

# The Skill of Self Confidence

You may have heard of someone called Dr. Ivan Joseph. He is a respected university soccer coach in the USA. In one of his TedX talks, he speaks about what he looks for in a player.

The first things he looks for in any individual are self-confidence and self-belief. Of course there are many other things to consider, but they are secondary to the above. Whether the doctor accepts a student and awards them a scholarship depends on these things.

In short, he needs to know how they perceive themselves. For Dr. Joseph, they must have total faith and belief in their ability to succeed. Their current skill level, at this stage, is not as important as their self-belief.

Or at the very least they must have the "potential" to have total faith and belief in their ability to succeed. Dr. Joseph is able to identify any potential when he interviews the candidates.

Dr. Ivan Joseph defines confidence like this:

*"It's the skill of believing in one's ability to perform an act or reach a desired result despite the odds, the difficulty, or the adversity."*

He goes on to say that no matter how strong or how fast a player is; these physical features won't serve him or her well if the belief in one's self was absent.

He explains his idea with the following thoughts:

*"When we lose sight or lose belief in ourselves, then we will end up achieving nothing."*

I recommend you search for his TEDx speech on YouTube. Just type: Dr. Ivan Joseph - The Skill of Self Confidence – TED.

# The Importance of Mental Strength

You can measure how mentally strong a team is by its players. The ones to pay particular attention to are the Regista and the two center backs.

Go through all the strong, A-Class soccer teams that you know, or know of, and you will see what I mean.

In most cases, 90 percent of these teams will have one thing in common. That is, they all have at least one central midfielder who has a special personality. It is one that combines self-confidence and natural leadership. Let's look at a few examples.

Think of the German midfielder, Philip Lahm. Another good example is the Spanish midfielder, Xabi Alonso. Others include the English midfielders Steven Gerrard, Paul Scholes, Roy Keane and Patrick Vieira.

Let's not forget too, Zinedine Zidane, Didier Deschamp and Andrea Pirlo. Even more examples are Francesco Totti and Daniele De Rossi. All these guys are/were midfielders and all had/have the confidence to lead their teams to lots of victories.

If you don't have these attributes, just tell yourself that you don't have them – yet. There are ways that you can build your own self-confidence. Having confidence in yourself also helps you to develop your leadership skills.

Your physical abilities will also improve further. It's sad to say, but self-confidence is something that so many players struggle to find. So the question for you is this:

*"How can I improve my self-belief and self-confidence?"*

Those of you who have watched the video mentioned above will already know the answer to that. Still, let's write these things down too. This way you also have reference to them in this book.

Building your confidence comes down to two basic things. Those are repetition and affirmations. We will start by looking at the importance of repetition in some detail.

# The Importance of Repetition

To begin this, you will first have to identify your mistakes and weak points. Whatever these are, they are your problem. As you know, it's not possible to apply a solution to anything until you first know what the problem is.

Once you have identified your problem areas you need to zoom in and work hard at fixing them. So what might be the kind of things that are holding you back?

Well, it could be one of many, but in most cases they will be quite typical. For example, you might lack in some skill and that's affecting your confidence.

If so, then you have to work over and over until you have improved it (repetition). When you can do something well you become confident. When you can't, you are insecure and lack confidence. *Truly agree!*

You might now be thinking something like this:

*"Hang on a minute, I have tried to improve my skill but I just can't get any better at it."*

If this is the case, then there are two things at play here. One is that you have convinced yourself that you won't get any better. If this is true, then you're right, you won't. That is, unless you change your attitude toward it.

The second thing is that you probably try to improve the skill by doing the same thing over and over. You see, repetition cannot be effective if the approach is all wrong. In this case, then of course you won't get any better.

In other words, you need to approach it from a different angle. After all, what you're doing is obviously not working.

In the TEDx talk with Dr. Joseph (see above), he gives an example of one of his goalkeepers. This guy, despite being physically capable, had a problem with catching the ball.

No matter how hard he tried, the ball would almost always slip through his fingers. There was nothing wrong with his hands or his eyesight, but the more he tried, the more he failed. What happened was that he'd convinced himself that he was useless when it came to catching a soccer ball.

Now is a good time to repeat the wise words of Henry Ford:

*"Whether you think you can, or you think you can't, you're right on both counts."* It's all about believing.

OK, let's look at how Dr. Joseph approached the problem with the goalie that couldn't catch.

Under the instruction of Dr. Joseph, this wannabe goalkeeper began his repetition training. His task was to kick the ball against a wall and catch it on the rebound, or at least try to catch it. He was to do this 350 times a day for eight consecutive months.

Simple repetition was the method used here, nothing more. So did he make it, did he overcome his belief that he was useless when it came to catching a soccer ball? Well, let's just say he found his confidence and went on to play at a professional level in Europe. For him, what must have once seemed like an impossible dream had become his reality.

*Wow! Inspiring!*

So, for you to duplicate this approach you should find out what you are not so good at and work hard at fixing it. Remember, it's not only about repetition. It's about using repetition in a way that helps, not hinders, your progress.

So if you have been practicing in a certain way and not getting any better, then you need to change your approach. If you're not sure how, then get advice from someone who's more experienced. There's nothing wrong with asking for a little guidance to help get you off on the right path.

Let's look at an example. Maybe you're not good at headers. In this case, get someone to send you crosses from different positions and sides of the field.

Put fixed signs on the goal and point your headers toward them. Do this every night after you finish your regular training session. Keep at it for six months, or even 12 months if you need to.

Don't allow frustration or failed attempts to put you off. Look at them and ask yourself why you failed. In other words, use failures and setbacks as learning tools. Just keep at it, and stay positive. Always remember that you will become confident at headers in corners and fouls as long as you believe.

Let's take another example. Let's say you are not good at passes, both long and short. The way to develop this skill is to place cones all over the field and hit them with your passes. You need to do this from different areas, different angles and with varying power. Again, the most important thing you have to tell yourself is this:

I will improve as long as I commit to the long term and never give up trying. I know this because repetition is a proven technique. Repetition can work for anyone who follows through with it.

Taking fouls is another area that knocks the confidence out of a lot of players. If you can relate, observe the professionals. See how they play and then try to mimic their style. Keep at it for as long as you need to. As long as you practice the right way, you will become better and more confident in your ability.

Andrea Pirlo is one of the best free kick takers in the world. He once wrote in a book that he mastered playing fouls after watching and mimicking the Brazilian free kick master, Juninho Pernambucano. He revealed that he continued to make many mistakes along the way.

But because of his belief in the power of repetition, he never gave up. Eventually, he learned what he needed to do. Because of his patience and persistence, he went on to become the exceptional free-kick taker that he is today.

And finally we have tackling and marking opponents to consider. If you're having trouble in these areas, train more. I would suggest you train with both younger and older teams, if you can, beyond your regular practice. Keep this up until you're good at what you lack in.

To summarize on the repetition technique:

Find out what you're bad at and get advice on how to fix it. It is then up to you to take positive action. Remember to keep things simple, not fancy. Embrace the power of repetition until you get to where you need to be. If you do this, I can promise you that you will succeed.

Whatever area or areas need improvement, use the repetition technique to zoom in and focus on them. Repetition is the mother of skill. Constant repetition carries conviction. This works, it really does work, providing that is, you stick to the plan.

① Identify your mistakes. Set a schedule for practice. Repetition makes great. Repeat and learn from mistakes. Then Repeat...

## Affirmations

Now we will take a look at affirmations. All these are is positive statements that describe a desired situation. The approach is a simple one.

All you need to do is repeat them over and over. Most would agree that this is best done out loud, until they get impressed on the subconscious mind. What you're doing here is feeding your brain with positive messages.

The idea is to keep doing this until you believe these statements to be true. In your case, these affirmations need to be specific statements. By that, I mean they should relate to your problem areas. When practiced often, affirmations will help you to overcome self-sabotaging, negative thoughts and beliefs.

*[handwritten: Id. ok.]*

Muhammad Ali, the greatest boxer of all time, once said:

*"I am the greatest. I said that before I knew I was."*

This is the type of thing you should be telling yourself, but with more specific statements. Anything less and you will get less.

Understand that belief is something which works both ways. We've already seen that in the Henry Ford quote above. Just know that you are only ever able to excel in something when you believe it's achievable.

Likewise, you will never be able to achieve something if you think it's impossible. In other words, you're right on both counts.

So if you believe that you are just average or mediocre, guess what? You will never be anything other than average or mediocre. Your belief system is a very powerful thing.

If you can identify with having self-doubts, then affirmations can help. You will want to find or create some powerful and positive affirmations that are specific to you.

*[handwritten notes: 1) well. But sometimes y are just cant put VERY high standards that are not realistic. I cant practice 8 hours when I only have 4. Being realistic is key too.]*

183

*Set high expectations that you can reach and slowly raise the bar. I want to become the best and believe that I can be the best. It just takes time.*

See, quite often, people don't always know the difference between true and false. It's important to understand the difference between can and can't; what is, and is not achievable. Let me explain what I mean.

There are some things we can't do because they are impossible for us for whatever reason(s). There are other things that we can't do that are possible but we think they're impossible.

There is a big difference here. Just because you don't think you can do a thing, that doesn't mean you can't. It just means you think you can't. But if you always think that way, then you will never change.

Unless that is, you approach things with an open mind, even if you don't believe. So if you think it's impossible to change your view, then you can fake it till you make it. Yes, faking is something else that also works.

This not only applies to soccer, but to life in general. If you're still skeptical about this approach, my advice is simple: never knock something new until you've at least tried it for yourself.

Most people think they can't do something because they have convinced themselves they can't. Either that or someone has influenced them enough for them to think that way.

Even though you don't know it, you have been using affirmations all along. The problem is you've been telling yourself you can't do something. You know the kind of thing.

You might feed yourself messages like: "Oh, I'm no good at this." Or maybe you even curse yourself for being useless. These things are not likely true, but to you they are real and meaningful.

Aha!

So what you've been doing, in effect, is feeding your mind with negative affirmations. How is this so? Well, when you tell yourself something often enough, you end up believing it.

Positive affirmations work in the exact same way. The only difference here is that you're using affirmations for positive purpose, not negative. If the negative ones have been successful, then surely the positive ones must work too, but in the other direction.

You don't need a degree in rocket science to build a new belief system. Whatever you repeat the most is what the subconscious mind ends up believing to be true. It really is that straightforward. You might be thinking that this is just too simple to be effective.

Don't let the simplicity of this approach deter you. It is a technique that works, and there is scientific evidence to back this up.

All kinds of people use positive affirmations to help change their life for the better. If you want changes in your own belief system, you now know how to do it.

Affirmations are only half of the solution though. Thinking without doing won't help. By that, I mean it's no good believing you're great at goal kicks, for example, if you don't get out there and prove yourself right.

When you believe you can do a thing, then achieving it becomes so much easier. So whatever you do, remember to act on your thoughts. That's positive thoughts, not negative.

That's why religion is effective.

People have different mindsets. Some mindsets help, others hinder or halt a person's development. The reasons for this are many. Scientists and researchers have tried to explain the phenomenon of the different mindsets.

They have finally drawn some conclusions on this. They believe people have one of two mindsets, at varying degrees. One is what they call the Growth Mindset, and other is the Fixed Mindset. Keep reading to find out which of these you have.

② Posibive affirmations. Remind yourself that good things are coming. If you coneb it with work. Good, positive self talk ☺

## The Growth Mindset

Someone who has a "growth mindset" is positive in nature. They tend to believe they can build on their most basic abilities, and so they do. Their simple approach is dedication and hard work, driven by belief.

They are generally upbeat and have a positive attitude and outlook upon life in general. People with a growth mindset have within them a genuine love of learning. In essence, they have a resilience that is essential for great accomplishment.

People who succeed in soccer only achieve their goals because of their mindset. Look at all the soccer greats for example. You will find that most of them have the qualities associated with the growth mindset.

This is the mindset that creates motivation and productivity. This not only applies to soccer but to all sports. It applies to business and education too. People with this kind of mindset also tend to have good relationships with their fellows.

To sum up the growth mindset:

People who have, or develop, a growth mindset are happier, healthier and have a real zest for living. They embrace new challenges, knowing that they will come out stronger on the other side.

## The Fixed Mindset

Let's take a look at the fixed mindset and the difference between it and the growth mindset. People with a fixed mindset tend to think more than they act. They know what they can do but rarely stretch themselves past a certain level.

They will acknowledge their basic qualities but that's usually where it stops. These types dread failure so they avoid it by not trying. *Used to be me too.*

They feel that talent on its own is enough to succeed. They also think that talent is something that other people are blessed with, but not them.

They're wrong, of course, because talent alone is never enough to succeed at anything. But the belief system of those with a fixed mindset is so inflexible. This makes it hard or impossible to convince them of anything outside of their fixed beliefs.

I'm sure you have heard the saying that someone is "stuck in their ways." Well, that is typical of a fixed mindset personality. It's sad to say, but true nonetheless, that people of this mindset belong in the all-talk and no-action category. They often say they are going to do something, but never actually do it.

*[handwritten margin notes: "used to be like that", "Not anymore", smiley face]*

187

*This all applies to me in the past. I'm now trying my best to become a different person at everything and I can already feel the diff.*

They usually have a lowly opinion of themselves in general, even though they might not admit it. They worry a lot about their traits. With a fixed mindset it's hard to deal with criticism, even when it's constructive. In short, a fixed mindset suggests limited negative thinking patterns.

Can you identify as having a fixed mindset? If yes, then don't get too despondent. The good news is that can change your conviction through various exercises.

There are lots of books written on the subject too. But to sum it up in brief, here is the crux of what you need to do to shift from a negative, fixed mindset, to a positive, growth mindset.

## Listen to Your Fixed Mindset "Voice"

That headline might sound weird, but it's not, as I will now explain. This is the quiet voice that tells you that something is impossible. I guess it's more of a thought than a voice.

But whatever you want to call it, this is something that communicates with you. It is the voice that says you can't do a thing. It then justifies itself by having you come up with 101 reasons why this is true.

The first thing for you to do is to recognize this voice when it speaks. Understand that YOU are not your mind. Your mind is a part of who you are, just like any other body part.

That means you can learn to control it. When you say you can't do something, it's not you coming to a well thought out conscious conclusion. It is your mind telling you that you can't. Your mind tells you these things because of the fixed, negative mindset.

The second thing you need to do is acknowledge the fact that you have choices. So far you have chosen to believe a lot that is negative and haven't disputed this.

You have become so used to it, that it's become a natural behavior for you. This is something that tends to happen at the subconscious level. You can now choose NOT to believe your fixed-mindset at the conscious level.

From now on you get to choose to develop your growth-mindset. The way you do this is simple, but it might take a while before positive changes start to materialize. So the sooner you start on this, the better.

OK, so the way you begin to make these changes to you mindset is by refusing to accept what the fixed mindset tells you.

Whenever your inner voice tells you, "No, you can't," turn things around by saying, "Oh yes I can." It's that simple, but like I said, it might take a while. This exercise is all about listening to your internal voices and adjusting your thinking. Fake it till you make it in the beginning, if you need to.

The final thing you need to do is get used to hearing both voices, fixed and growth. When you hear the fixed voice, replace it with how the growth mindset would talk to you in the same situation.

You then need to take action because thinking alone won't serve you well. For example, say you're having a tough time passing the ball.

The old fixed mindset might tell you that it's because you've reached the limits of your potential. It tells you that this is as good as you're likely to get, so QUIT trying to improve. Usually you would heed this voice, but not anymore.

This is the kind of old stinking thinking that you're trying to get rid of. Now consciously bring in your growth mindset to counteract what the fixed mindset has just told you.

Your growth mindset will tell you that there's lots of room for improvement. It suggests you look at other ways to develop, and maybe you could ask for help from those more experienced. You choose to listen to the growth mindset and take fresh action.

There will come a point where you don't have to think about what a growth mindset would say. This is because it will eventually take over and become your normal way of thinking and dealing with situations.

For now though, your fixed mindset is your default way of thinking. That means you have to counteract it by forcing the growth mindset to take over.

And you do this by replacing the negative thoughts with positive ones. What you're doing here is waking up the growth mindset.

Just start by giving yourself alternative options. These are usually the total opposite to what the fixed mindset suggests. So if your fixed mindset says, "No, you can't," replace that with "Yes I can, and I will." I'm sure you get the idea.

Recipe for Success.

You must remember to always take positive action on positive thoughts. If you get into the habit of doing this, your growth mindset will kick in sooner rather than later.

I say again, this is something that may take a while, depending on how fixed your mindset has become. So the sooner you start, the quicker you get to transform.

If you need more help, there are plenty of good books and articles online that will guide you through the entire process in great detail.

## Take Responsibility

You can increase your confidence by taking full responsibility for everything that happens to. For every action, or inaction, on the field there are consequences. Sometimes these will be good, other times bad. When you take responsibility over all that happens you get to leverage your performance. It's true.

Think of it like this:

When you are the problem you can also become the solution. If somebody else is the problem (or the cause of it), then you have no solution, or at least you cannot control it in the same way. Whatever happens happens.

But if you lost the ball, or messed up a certain play, there will be a reason for that. It might just be that the opponent was a better player. It might also be because you made a wrong decision.

Whatever it was, it happened because of something. If that something was a blatant foul by an opponent, then perhaps it was out of your control. In a case like this, everyone will know what happened and no further explanation is necessary.

But if it was something else, then perhaps you could have done something different to avoid it. If so, then own up to that.

It is only when you identify your shortcomings that you get to change. Maybe you weren't fast enough, motivated enough, or strong enough. If you can see these shortcomings, and then own them, you can then get to look at things in a different light. It's too easy to pass our own failings onto other people. It's often preferable, or at least that's how it might seem at the time.

Yet a little humility can work wonders when things don't go according to plan. I can understand how it's not a nice feeling to admit you messed up.

But I also know that those who do, then go on to become much stronger, better-rounded players. And by the way, admitting to your mistakes is not the same as putting yourself down.

*Very good statem.*

In fact, there's a huge difference between the two, and you must avoid the latter at all costs. I've emphasized a few times in this book the importance of embracing failures.

You need to look at them as something to learn from, not shun. Once you can do this your performance will improve and your confidence will grow.

The reason for this is simple. When you blame others you are passing the buck; you're denying responsibility. And when you pass the buck you are not in control.

It really is impossible to be in control of your game when you don't own it. It is only when you feel in control that you get to be confident. The consequence of that is a marked improvement in the way you feel and function on the field.

It's important to understand one thing. That is, you can never feel confident or in control when you blame someone or something else for your faults. It just can't happen.

Self-belief and self-confidence are what will take you far. This not only applies to soccer, but your life in general. Confidence makes you brave on the field and will have your opponents fear you.

No matter what happens during the game, or how bad your performance is on the day, you must stay confident.

If you don't feel it, you can at least fake it and convey confidence. You do this until the last play and the final whistle. It's not difficult for others to spot any lack of confidence in someone. And when they do, they use it to their advantage. In fact, the bullying types feed off this. strong person.

It takes a real man to own up to his mistakes on the field. Those who blame something or someone else for their blunders are afraid to lose face. Loosing face is a term that suggests you become humiliated or not respected.

This is why so many players don't like to admit their failures. But I can promise you that this kind of thinking is all wrong. It is something that will only hinder, never help, your development.

Taking Responsibility is an important principle. When you do it with sincerity, it earns you great respect, not disrespect, as some tend to think. When you own your faults, you also accept the responsibility to improve.

You are, in fact, conveying a message to your teammates. You are saying that what happened was not good and you will do your level best to make sure it doesn't happen again.

This is a measure of your self-worth. It shows your level of security. It is a true sign of strength and courage.

So as you can see, having the ability to own your mistakes on the field empowers you. It helps you to grow in ways that bring about great rewards and accomplishments. This is not only true in your game, but in your life more generally.

Understand that a lot of the contest between you and your opponents is pure mind games. Just know that confidence is your most important tool in the battle of the minds.

Practice and repeat. Your Adopt a growth midset. Embrace "failures" or mistakes and learn from tcm.

Take responsibility for your mistakes. get better. Never put down yourself. 😊

194

# 26. Not Having a Fixed Visualization Routine

Before we begin, let's get clear on two things:
1. If you can't dream it, you won't get it.
2. All great players are into visualization.

It's important to never underestimate the power of visualization. I'm serious. This is one of the greatest mind exercises you have at your disposal. Visualization is a technique that many athletes and soccer players use to enhance their performance.

Soccer players who practice visualization are able to achieve greater things on the field than those who don't. This is not a replacement for hard work, of course. It is a contribution to your overall training program.

There are two main reasons for you to perform visualization. The first is that it prepares you so that you can perform at your best. The second is that it's free. It takes no effort, no money, and no resources. Let's look at this in more detail.

## Visualization Prepares You

It helps you to predict new scenarios. With visualization you can prepare for whatever new happens to you or to your team during the game. Anytime you visualize yourself performing well you're helping your brain.

You are preparing it to identify and deal with any obstacles that may come your way. These are things that might have otherwise gotten in your way if you hadn't visualized them beforehand. When you can do this, you have more chance of an outstanding performance.

Visualization also enhances your decision making process. You are better able to make fast and more accurate decisions. Your reflexes are quicker too.

All these thing and more become possible to you when you visualize them. This is because you have rehearsed them over and over inside your mind. In other words, you have prepared for all eventualities.

## Visualization Is Free and Easy

Bet of all is that visualization will not exhaust you. You can do it anytime and anywhere. It takes almost no energy and you will not experience any physical fatigue.

## Don't Knock It till You Try It

There is no easier way to increase your success than to visualize it. Some skeptics think that it's too easy and because of that it can't be true. My advice to you is to ignore the naysayers. It is the sheer simplicity of this approach that puts a lot of people off. But why knock something without first trying it?

After all, it takes little time and zero resources. You've heard the saying: If something is too good to be true then it probably is. This is why a lot of people write it off as some kind of hoax. There is even science to back up the effectiveness of this technique.

Despite this, the naysayers are still not convinced. All I know is that anyone who is resistant to visualization techniques are missing out big time. Like I said earlier, it's never a good idea to knock something until you have tried it for yourself. And when it comes to visualization, there's nothing to lose but a bit of your time.

# Wayne Rooney and Visualization

You have most likely heard of the famous Man United attacker, Wayne Rooney. What you may not know is that Rooney uses visualization to help improve his performance.

In an interview once, he revealed just how his visualization routine helps him. In fact, he attributed his visualization to the many great goals he has scored over time.

And if you're familiar with Rooney, you will know that he has scored a lot of stunning goals during his career. You should be able to find most of them easy enough on video sharing websites like YouTube.

OK, let's look at Rooney's routine.

He would spend the whole night before the game visualizing events on the field. When I say visualize, I mean he would really focus on the details.

For example, he would be playing in the exact kit he'd be wearing on the day. The rival side would also be in their colors and the fans in the grandstands.

Rooney would see everything, just how it would look on the day. He would perform well against the opposition and go on to score some great goals for his side. He would also make some impressive moves and triumph in challenging situations.

Rooney explained that the reason behind his visualizing was simple. It was so that he could mentally prepare himself for every single eventuality. He knows how games play out, and that helps him to anticipate and zoom in on the details.

I do /did all the time!
I's an amazingly helpful technique.

He said that his visualization acts as a kind of "game memory." This "game memory," as he calls it, is are the last visualizations embedded into his mind.

Rooney went on to say that visualization helped him to score some of the most amazing goals early on in his career. Because of it, he was able to hit far posts from 30 yards, and sometimes more.

He also got to perform Messi type tricks. You know the kind of thing, dribbling through many opponents in a single play. None of this, Rooney suggests, would have been possible without visualization.

So powerful is visualization that soccer players and athletes use it regularly. It is as an integral part of their training strategy. They only do it because it's easy and effective, and that's about it. If it didn't work, they would bother. Tens of thousands of sports stars can't be wrong.

When a soccer player visualizes, he gets to translate his positive visualizations into positive actions on the field.

And these visualization exercises don't need to be complex or time consuming to become effective. I would suggest something like 20-30 minutes a day, and maybe twice that time the night before a game. That's it.

It's important not to confuse visualization with day dreaming or fantasizing. It's nothing of the kind. With visualization you are envisaging how real events might actually play out.

You then visualize how you intend to deal with them if and when they materialize. Your visualizations must always be positive and in your favor. Put another way, you are always the star of the show.

Before you begin your visualization sessions, make sure you know what your goals are. I would suggest you write stuff down beforehand, especially in your early sessions.

Once you know how you need to perform in various situations, sit back, relax, and play them over in your head.

# The Importance of Clarity

When you visualize with good focus it provides you with clarity. Having a clearness of mind lets you unleash latent skills and capabilities. These are often attributes that you never knew you had.

By visualizing, you get focus much better. This means you get to make smarter use of your attention, your energy, and your time.

Put another way, you waste less time on the unimportant things and spend more time on what's most important. Clarity allows you to track and process everything around you. It helps you to avoid obstacles because you are now able to see things from a higher perspective. I'm not kidding here. Visualization is the most empowering mind-technique for any player who wants to improve his game. It's not only useful in sports either.

Successful people, from all walks of life, use visualization on a regular basis. They do not use it in the hope that it will work, they practice it because it does work. It provides them with real clarity. This is something which is sadly lacking in today's busy world. In fact, most modern lifestyles have stripped us of this once common quality.

There are just too many distractions and external temptations in life these days. They kill the dreams of many aspiring soccer players too. This is why it's so important to clear the clutter from the mind and replace the space with clear, simple focus. This is what visualization helps you to do.

Most of you reading here will know nothing of a different time. This is because you were either born at the tail end of the twentieth century or in the Twenty-first century.

Living and lifestyles have changed a lot, just ask anyone of grandparent age. And because of these changes, many people nowadays have a limited focus span. At least compared to how it used to be they do.

Every single day things move on, cease to be, or become altered. Because of this, it can seem impossible sometimes to focus on anything for too long at a time.

One moment you place your focus on one thing and the next on something else. Heck, it's no wonder stress has become the curse of this new millennium.

Everyone who has ever lived on earth has a limited focus span.

201

For all these reasons and more, you need to see your goals before you achieve them. You have to hardwire your game plan into your mind, and visualizations help you to do just that. With clarity comes the elimination of chaos, confusion and turmoil.

If you're ready for positive change, then the time has come to put a stop to all the everyday stuff that gets in the way. Now is the time to step back from the usual routine and ignite your focus. It's time now to visualize what you want from your soccer career so that you pursue it.

*very Insp. vation*

Your hopes and dreams to excel at soccer will always be just hopes and dreams without a plan of action. The only way to get what you want is with real clarity, and that is something you can claim with visualization.

*I am a visualization master already. It takes me to a new world! Its like living a different life*

# 27. Not Knowing How Contain a Counter Attack for DMs, CMs

The best way to contain an attacker is to force him to move toward the side line. This approach is even more useful when you're outnumbered or in a counter attack. It is certainly a better approach than going deep inside the penalty area or its edge.

Let's look at the best way to approach this.

- Position yourself in a way that blocks all possible passes or predicted runs.

- Ask for help from another teammate. One of you will apply the pressure while the other waits to intercept the pass. Note that your teammate should be cautious. He must be confident about getting the ball. If he fails, there will be serious danger to your goal, especially if no one is guarding your goal area at the time. If taking the ball looks too risky, then pause. In this case, let the attacker come to you. If you get out of the game and he passes you, it's almost a breakaway.

- Be willing to cover for any player whenever needed. For example, let's say a long through pass gets played toward the side of your penalty area. And let's also say your center back decides to go after the ball. He does this to pressure the ball holder on the flank. But by going after the ball, he also leaves an empty spot in the penalty area. What should you do? You cover his back, and without any delay. You do this by taking his position inside the penalty area. From there you wait for any cross to be played in case your teammate fails to get the ball from the rival attacker.

- If a player runs behind you and waits for the ball, forget about him. Your focus needs to be on the player facing you. The guy behind you is the responsibility of someone else on your team.

- Never take your eyes off the ball. By that I mean don't focus on the attacker or his legs. It's the ball you're after, so it's the ball you need to fix your eyes on.

- Always prepare yourself for making a tackle. Don't be afraid to send the ball outside the field for a throw-in or a corner. This way is much better than conceding a goal.

- If you already have one yellow card, stick to your position. Let another teammate, who hasn't been booked yet, go after the attacker whenever possible. The reason is that he may have to perform a foul against the opponent. This is something you just can't risk. As you know, a second yellow card means you're out of the game.

- Be sensitive with your feet and prepare to close your legs quickly. Why would you want to do this? Well, it's because the favored way of moving past a defender is to send the ball between his legs.

- Watch videos for the rival winger before the game starts. Observe how he deals with defenders in counter attacks.

- When you tackle or slide, make sure you touch the ball before the opponent does. This is so he doesn't get awarded a foul or a penalty, and also to prevent you from getting booked.

- Don't slide unless you're in the perfect position to reach the ball. Sliding for the sake of it can cause you and your team all kinds of unnecessary problems.

- The more determined you are at extracting the ball, the better chance you have of getting it.

In the next chapter we will look at how playmakers and wingers can best implement a counter attack.

# 28. Not Knowing How to Benefit from a Counter Attack – for Wingers and Playmakers

Having an excellent fitness levels and stamina throughout the entire 90 minutes is essential. It is something that will help you deal with counter attacks. In general, the success of these counter attacks relies mostly on your speed to react to them.

OK, below are the points you need to keep in mind.

- Once you receive the ball you should not waste a second trying to control it. Keep all your focus on either running with the ball or moving it quickly to the front. Remember, the quality and the speed of your pass is what makes a counter attack so dangerous.
- When you hold the ball as you wait for an attacker to get into a better position, PAUSE for a moment. Wait until the rival defender moves toward you. When he does that, that's time to pass the ball over to your teammate. You do this just before he blocks the passing angle.
- Never shoot the ball when you have a better alternative option. Most of the time, the player leading the counter attack will be the farthest of his attacking teammates from the goal.
- If you're running with the ball on the wing, don't pass it too early. Instead, wait until you enter the penalty area and get closer to the goal if you can. This is the best time to pass the ball on to your nearest teammate.
- Just make sure to keep your pass a safe distance from the goalkeeper's body. If you play the ball too close to the keeper, he has a better chance to intercept it. The best way to prevent this from happening is to play the ball diagonally, and toward any of your teammates coming from behind. Note that these guys are not usually marked.

- If you only have one or two defensive players to contend with, try to get past them and make a run to the front. This move will confuse the rival defender for a moment and catch him off guard. This should give you a couple of valuable extra seconds; just enough to out run him at least.
- Unless you're a winger, try not to move toward the corner. A smart defender may push you toward the corner so that he can restrict your movements. It's a common tactic which is used to hold you back. Rival defenders do this to give their backup players time to come and block you from any shooting opportunity you might have had.
- If you're a DM or CM, and feel that you have the opportunity to add to a counter attack, don't hesitate. Always feel free to take part in the attack if the situation is right. Many great defensive midfielders get to score this way. You just need to be smart enough to know when to advance and when to stick to your position. This is something that will change with different situations and teams or course.

# 29. Not Considering Becoming the Best

Did you know that the basis of every team relies on having four key players on the side? It's true, and as you read on you will understand why. First off, let's look at who these four essential players are.

They consist of a strong goalkeeper, a sneaky attacker, a tough defender and a talented playmaker. That's about it. Give any good coach these four plyers and he can work miracles.

The former Scottish soccer manager, Sir Alex Ferguson, is proof of this. Ferguson managed to win league titles with a group of average players. There were even times when his team had to play with a few below average players on the side.

At least on a professional level they were below average. He could do this because he was still able to put together a good top four in the crucial positions (see above). The guys he had at his disposal were:

Edwin Van der Sarr (GK), Rio Ferdinand (CB), Wayne Rooney in the front, and both Paul Scholes and Michael Carrick in the middle.

You might be wondering why I'm bothering to mention this. Well, it's because I want you to realize that A—class midfielders are both rare and valuable. Big teams pay big bucks to have any of these guys.

You can judge a team's performance and their ability to win trophies and championships by knowing who plays on that team's central line. This is especially so with the defensive midfielder. You can do this even before looking at the qualities of the team manager.

The difference between unsuccessful coaches and successful ones is obvious. Take Jose Mourinho as an example. Jose knows just what he needs to do to control the tempo of a game.

And the way he does that is by having a pair of excellent central midfielders on side, like the ones he now has at Chelsea. They are Nemanja Matich, and the Spanish assisting machine Cesc Fabregas.

Fact: Average goals lead to average actions and eventually an average life.

Think small and you will get small. Think BIG and you will achieve great things as long as you act on your goals. If you want to be noticed, you cannot, you must not, allow your goals to be shallow and limited.

If you do, you will just get to play for some team, make some money, and buy some nice things, and not much else. You can achieve stuff like that with a normal 9-5 job.

Instead you should aim as high as your mind can take you. If soccer is in your blood, don't let anything or anyone convince you that you can't reach your dreams. Set goals bigger than you can imagine and have very high expectations of yourself.

The most important thing of all is to always put soccer first. It should always be about the game, above all the spoils that a successful career may bring with it. They will materialize if you get good anyway, but they should never be your key motivating factor.

# Develop a Winning Attitude

This is a good time for me to introduce you to the 10X rule. This is something that I push a lot in my books. I do this because it's a powerful and effective approach to developing a winning mindset.

*The 10X rule?*

Yes, it's a book, but not just any book. This has to be one of the best books ever written about success and attaining a winning mindset. It's by an American Multimillionaire salesman, Grant Cardone. His book is popular the world over, and for very good reason too.

I wouldn't be telling you about this book if I hadn't read it myself. I have also experienced the principles it contains firsthand. I have read this book cover to cover many times in the past and will continue to read it. In fact, I seem to get more out of it each time I do just that. I recommend that you do the same.

This isn't just another one of those self-help books from some self-confessed inspirational coach. This is a motivational and practical program for success. It is by someone who has succeeded in real life.

Many inspirational coaches have not succeeded in the real world. They just tell others how they should do it. The 10X Rule is far better than anything else I have ever come across, and it's a real page turner too, which always helps.

*Who is Grant Cardone and why should I care?*

Grant Cardone is a New York Times bestselling author, international speaker, and business innovator. He is a leading social media personality. Cardone is the top sales trainer in the world today. He holds a huge multifamily real estate portfolio throughout the United States.

Grant Cardone teaches the real principles of self-belief. These are things that you can carry into every facet of your life, including your approach to soccer. If you need a motivational boost then this is the book for you.

I've read quite a few books of this genre in my time, and this is by far the best. It is a fresh approach that will inspire you to raise your standards so that you can go on to achieve great things.

This is the only book you will ever need to deal with motivational issues. I'm not an affiliate for this book, so you won't find any links from me taking you to some checkout page. I recommend it because I, and many others, have changed parts of our life for the better because of it. You should be able to find the 10X Rule easy enough on Amazon and other online book stores.

If you decide to get a copy (recommended), then I suggest you read this book over and over. And keep going over it until the principles of the 10X Rule embed deep inside your mind. When this does happen, and it will, the way you think, feel, and function will change forever.

After you have read it through once or twice you will understand. If you do this you will appreciate why so many people call this "The Encyclopedia of Success." The 10X Rule is what you need to develop the same work ethic of players like Cristiano Ronaldo and Paolo Maldini.

## The Approach of the 10X Rule

The thing I like most about this book is the approach. Its main message is not just about the importance of goal setting, it's about how high you set those goals. The idea is to set and aim for huge, goals.

That means goals that border on the ridiculous, at least compared to what you have been used to. This is not pure fantasy; it is an approach that works and works well. The idea is that setting these huge goals will give you impetus. It's an approach that will see you take more action and achieve more results than you ever thought possible. Let me explain.

OK, so you might already be thinking that this is an approach which is unrealistic. It's not, and hundreds of thousands of people have benefited from this. I too thought it was a bit "pie in the sky" at first, but not anymore. Any of you who are familiar with my work will know how I always talk of the importance of setting realistic goals.

But when I talk about being "realistic," I am referring to the mini goals, or checkpoints. These are the targets you set to help you along the way. They are stepping stones, if you like. The ones that keep you focused as you journey toward your main, bigger goal. They are not the end goals, which should always be set high.

Everyone, to some degree, has self-doubts when venturing into the unknown. This is quite normal. The difference is that some players will allow those doubts to hold them back. Others players will push through them no matter what.

You must release yourself from the shackles of self-doubt if you are to thrive. It is only when you become free from this that you get to excel beyond your wildest dreams. This is where the 10X Rule comes to your rescue.

The author of the 10x rule suggests you make your goals huge. He talks about setting goals that are 10, 20 or even 50 times bigger than those you have set previous.

It might sound ridiculous, but it's not. The most ridiculous thing is the silly little goals that most people set for themselves. This is why there are more foot soldiers in society than winners and leaders.

In his book, Cardone also suggests using smaller, more achievable goals. He understands that this is the only way to reach your main target.

This is a logical and workable approach though it still takes commitment and hard work. Because your end goal is now much bigger and a lot grander, you will be keen to get there as soon as you can.

This means your mini goals will also be more ambitious. Even so, make sure that your smaller goals are still realistic; still achievable. They need to be challenging, of course, but doable nonetheless.

By making them a little tough, your efforts will intensify. Just know that small, mediocre, easy-to-achieve goals only result in mediocre progress. A lackluster approach will never lead to greater things.

A semi-ambitious approach produces semi-ambitious results. It's what often blocks a player's ability to excel and realize his full potential.

He often thinks he's doing his best, but in reality he could probably be doing so much more. The trouble is he doesn't always know it.

I will now use a hypothetical example to illustrate the point of aiming high.

Let's say that you have decided to start you own company and build yourself a profitable business. You start by setting yourself a main goal.

The aim of this new venture is to generate a decent income so that you get to improve your life and lifestyle. Now, which of the following two options would you prefer to end up with for your efforts?

-   **One**: A company worth $500,000 USD?
-   **Two**: A company worth $100,000,000 USD?

It doesn't take a genius to guess your answer. Of course you would want a successful $100,000,000 dollar company.

So you decide to set a high, ambitious goal and build a big company. You have now fixed your mind on creating a profitable $100m business. It's an ambitious goal but then you're an ambitious person. You would have a much different mindset if you had opted on building a much smaller concern.

But you haven't, so it's time to move forward with you massive plan of action. The chances are that you will be aggressive, ambitious and driven at all times.

You will have a lot more of each of these things than if you settled on creating a company worth just 500,000 USD.

You will feel different and you will function different as you get to work on the phases, or stepping stones. These are the mini goals that will help you to reach your end target. Your chance of succeeding is contingent on your thoughts and your actions.

Here's something to think about:

Let's say you set yourself a low, easily achievable goal. In this case, it is unlikely that you will ever exceed it. Put another way, if you believe you are only able to achieve something up to a certain level, you're right.

The fact is that the majority of people only ever dream about doing great things.

Or they might wish they could become what others have become. Alas, the dreaming stage is where most ambitious plans stop for many. In other words, dreamers do little more than fantasize about greatness.

They don't believe their dreams could ever come true, not for them at least, and so they never do. The sad thing is that many people could achieve so much more than they actually do, if only they had more belief in themselves. Let me expand on this a little.

If someone believes they can never become any better than they are, that doesn't mean they can't. It just means they think they can't. And in this case, they're absolutely right too, they can't.

At least not with their current mindset they can't. It's just not possible to achieve much when individuals place restrictions on themselves. The only way out of this mindset is if they unleash the real potential that lies within. And the only way to do that is to change their belief system.

If you talk to any great soccer player, he will always tell you that he sets himself big goals. If he didn't, he would never get to develop his skills to the levels he's reached. And the only reason he can aim high is because he has a genuine belief in himself.

This is the only way any of these players get to where they want to go. Even as young, enthusiastic boys, a long way off their dreams, they still held onto their beliefs. If they didn't believe, then they would never have made the grade. As I often point out, talent alone is futile unless it's followed up with positive action.

If you want to be up there with the world's best midfielders, then greatness has to be your end goal. Anything less and you will get less. That is something I can guarantee.

Starting today, take a good look at what your doubts might be. Tell yourself that the time has come to remove any restrictions that are holding you back. The next time you play with your team, either in a game or at a practice session, set higher standards for yourself.

In every game you play, aim to perform even better than you did in the game before it. Never accept that you are as good as you're likely to get. Remember this: if you just turn up and hope you'll do okay on the day, then your ability to excel will always lie dormant. Take this "higher goal" approach in everything that you do. That includes training sessions as well.

Again ask yourself this question:

Which is better for you as a soccer player: to take action toward the goal of becoming one of the best 10 players in your position, in the world. Or, opt for being the best player in your team, in your league or perhaps your country?

Settling for the latter is easier than the former, and it won't need you to exert yourself like the pros do. If you aim for the first goal though, then everything changes. This is where you strive to become one of the best 10 midfielders in the soccer world.

It will force you to develop a strong work ethic, much stronger than the easier goal. And even you happen to fall short on your bigger goal, all is not lost. You can almost be certain that you at least become the best in your region or even the country. Convinced?

Try this one. Next time you play with your team, set a much higher target for yourself, and I do mean a much higher target. Aim for something like creating 10-15 chances per game. Look to having 10 or 15 consecutive clean sheets, in the case where you're a defensive midfielder.

Remember, if you play it small you will achieve mediocre results at best. Try this more ambitious approach and leverage your focus. I can assure you that you will do better providing you are hungry for success. This is how big teams win big games and take home big trophies.

Let's look at an example. The dominant team, Bayern Munich, has a dominant coach, Pep Guardiola. These guys enter each game with the aim of coming away with more than just three points. They never settle for "good enough." They are always hungry for more, always wanting to score 7-8 goals per game.

In fact, Bayern Munich is the only team in Europe to have the highest number of goals scored per game. That's quite impressive when you think about it. I mean, they don't have star players on their side like the goal scoring machines Messi and Ronaldo.

What they do have, however, is a dedicated team that works well as a complete unit. Bayern Munich never assumes they are as good as they're likely to get, and they are exceptional too. But they always push for more of everything, and that's their strength.

Only you can determine your own success. You have to fall in love with the dream and give it the required effort to turn it into a reality. When you change the way you view yourself and your potential, then positive changes are inevitable.

You can learn from others and become inspired by a book like this. Yet none of it matters unless you take positive action toward greatness.

Ok, so you know what you need to do and what you need to avoid doing. To recap this chapter, I will end with a few facts that you might want to embed into you conscious mind.

First of all, don't set small goals or aim for small dreams. You can leave them to someone else. Understand that average dreams will always pull you down, never push you up. Being reasonably ambitious will never create enough motivation for you to grow.

Dream big, dream real big, and hold on to that dream. This is the one fundamental thing that you need to learn about success. It's only when you have big dreams and goals that your chances to achieve something extraordinary can happen.

I believe you are already motivated, and willing to do what it takes to become better. I say this because you have read this far down in the book.

It's now time to ramp up your motivation and work even harder than you are doing. Now is the time to set those big goals we've been looking at. It's time to release the potential you know you have. So set the goals that match your powers, your skills and your abilities.

You know the persistence that a six year old kid has when he tries to force his parents to buy him an ice cream. These little guys can be relentless sometimes, and they won't give in until they get what they want. And if they don't get it, everyone knows about it. But even if they fail, it does not deter them from trying again next time. You do need to take a lesson from the determination that many toddlers and youngsters have. Alas, this is something that many of us lose the older we get. I'm not talking about the tantrums, but the unrelenting determination. Now is the time for you to get that resolve back into your life.

So set yourself a 10X goal that relates to your career in soccer, and then just go for it. Make sure your approach is right and your determination is persistent. If you do this you will go on achieve great things. Not only will you do well, but your achievements will go beyond anything you could ever imagine.

Never lose sight of the fact that it's your responsibility to take action. How good you become depends on your desire to succeed.

# 30. You Drop the Gym

Here's something that you need to know. You won't ever reach a high level of physical strength, agility and speed with a weak body. The reason is because you need strength on the soccer field. Especially when playing as a wing player or a defensive midfielder.

This is not least because you have to make tens of tackles in each game. Some of these tackles will be against players who are bigger and stronger than you are. But your role aside, all soccer positions require physical strength and well-toned muscles.

Note that it's well-toned muscle and not muscular. We'll leave that to the body builders as it has no place on the soccer field. In fact, too much muscle only hinders the performance of a soccer player.

As you might know, there are some players who are not solid and nor do they have the muscle mass I'm referring to. Such players are unique and the exception to the rule. The winger Jesus Navas, who we looked at earlier, is one example.

There are many other examples, however, that prove why a lack in strength and muscle is not a good thing. If anything, it can be dangerous for the player. Let's take a look at some examples to prove the point.

## Vassiriki Abu Diaby

The former French player, Abou Diaby had a promising career ahead of him. He was all set to become the next Patrcik Viera (former Manchester City Midfielder). In fact, he was on track to be one of the best defensive midfielders in the history of soccer.

Unfortunately, Diaby wasn't strong enough to handle the beating that comes with this position. In total, he suffered 28 injuries in different parts of his body.

Because of this, he only got to play two games in the last three seasons. He now has no club to play for after his contract expired with Arsenal.

Diaby lost out on a magnificent career. The reason was because he didn't support his talent with enough physical strength. If only he had worked on this area he could have had a long and glowing career in the world of professional soccer.

# Eduardo Da Silva

You might have heard of Eduardo Da Silva, commonly known as Eduardo. His is a Brazilian-born Croatian attacker. Da Silva played for Arsenal between the years 2007 and 2010.

It's fair to say that he was one of the most skilled strikers I have ever seen. This is not just my opinion but that of many Arsenal fans too.

In fact, his coach, Arsene Wenger, believed he was one of the best strikers to ever play in the English club. This could have made him a club legend, but it wasn't to be. This is because Eduardo's career had a major setback.

He was the type of striker any soccer fan would love to see play for their team. Eduardo was fast, he was smart, and he always knew where to position himself when he played at Arsenal.

Best of all is that he knew how to finish. He was a great player, that's for sure, but I say "was" for a reason. You see, Da Silva had a major setback in that he wasn't solid and strong. This meant he was too fragile for the game.

In his first 27 games with Arsenal, Da Silva had scored 19 goals for the team. Besides this, he also had 12 assists to add to his sheet. Then, one day the inevitable happened. Da Silva suffered a sickening injury in a league game against Birmingham City.

The incident happened when City player, Martin Taylor, broke Eduardo's leg. It was in fact, one of the most shocking incidents in the history of the English premier league.

Without going into too much gory detail, Taylor caught Da Silva on the shin. As they collided, Taylor snapped Eduardo's fibula. The fibula is the outer of the two bones between the knee and the ankle. He also dislocated his left ankle.

Because of his injuries, Da Silva had no choice but to spend almost an entire year in the hospital. The medical team had a lot of work to do if they were to prepare him for a return to the game.

He made it back again in 2009, but never managed to regain his edge. Needless to say, his position as a leading attacker in the team became history. Da Silva left Arsenal after scoring only two goals in a total of eleven post injury games.

Eduardo Da Silva later spent four years in Ukraine playing for Shakhtar Donetsk. He's now playing for the Club do Flamengo in Brazil. Da Silva is just 32 years old.

So why am I bothering to mentioning this?

I'm using Da Silva's story as proof of what can happen to any player who doesn't take care of his build.

Da Silva was a high quality player. In fact, he could have become one of the best in the game. His mistake, and probably the Arsenal medical team's mistake as well, was not to work on his strength. Soccer is a demanding game. That means the players have to be in good physical condition at all times.

Fitness alone is never enough in soccer. You need all the joints to be strong and protected. The only way to do this is by having adequate muscle. For most players, this means it's necessary to spend time in the gym.

The fact is that accidents can, and sometimes do, happen to anyone. But having a strong physical body can protect you a lot against the falls and knocks that come with soccer. Even if you get injured, the chances are the injury will be less severe if you've got a bit of meat and muscle on your bones.

Furthermore, the recovery time will be less too, in most cases at least. Any serious player has an obligation. He owes it to himself, his team, and his fans to take good care of protecting himself against hurt and injury.

Da Silva's injury took a couple of years from his career, but that's not all it did. It also made him afraid and more cautious on his return to the game. He never got back to his full potential. He could no longer challenge defenders and attack the ball, not like he used to.

A strikers' performance declines faster than defenders and goalkeepers anyway. So losing so much time to a single injury was a devastating blow for Da Silva. On his return, it was quite easy for most defenders to steal a ball from him. It never used to be like that. It was also easy to win a physical challenge against him.

You can probably guess the reason why. It was because Da Silva had become nervous about getting hurt again. He was afraid of a repeat injury. You could even say that it's understandable under the circumstances.

# A Solid Body Allows You to Take on Different Roles

No matter what, you can't allow yourself to become a seasonal player if you want to be one of soccer's best midfielders. Seasonal players don't make it to be great players. Weak legs and muscles won't help you at all.

Four Rules to Increase Muscle

There are four basic rules that will allow help you to increase you strength and muscle. These rules relate to:

1. Protein intake
2. Lifting weights (the right way)
3. Knowing how far to go with muscle size
4. Doing multi-joint exercises

OK, so let's look at each of these in turn.

# Rule #1 - Spike up Your Protein Intake

Getting enough protein into your diet is an important rule. This is because physical activity breaks down muscle tissue. A midfielder certainly gets enough physical activity during a game. In actual fact, a professional soccer player can run from between 8-10 km on average, per game.

If the player doesn't get proper nutrition, then he can run into serious problems. In a worst case scenario, too much exertion and too little protein in the diet can put him into a state of catabolism. This occurs when the body starts to break down muscle tissue.

It does this to provide energy when there is no other source to fall back on. The body's primary source of energy comes from carbohydrates. Its secondary source is fat. The body's final, last resort energy source comes from muscle tissue. Note that using muscle tissue for energy is not a normal condition or a healthy one.

Your body will only start to use muscle tissue for energy under extreme conditions. For a soccer player, this occurs when he's not consuming enough calories over an extended period. So when a diet lacks nutritional value in some way, the body is unable to function as it should do under extreme conditions. Playing a full game of soccer is considered to be an extreme activity.

## How to Avoid Catabolism

The best way to avoid catabolism is to keep your body fueled with balanced amounts of protein. You might now be wondering what I mean by balanced amounts of protein. Don't worry, there is way to know whether you're getting enough protein or not. You can work this out using a simple calculation.

All you have to do is include at least 1.5 grams of protein per day for each one pound of your body weight. That's it. Protein is necessary as it helps to create amino acids inside your body.

Without getting too technical, amino acids are responsible for the muscle building process. They do this by repairing any damaged muscle fibers. This in turn, stops the breakdown and deterioration of muscle tissue.

## Rule #2 - When Lifting, Increase Weights and Decrease the Range of Your Repetitions

Remember your goal here is to tone up, not bulk up with big muscles. In other words, your aim is to increase your strength rather than your size. You so have to build some notable muscles to support your body against fractures and injuries. What you must not do is get too big.

The important thing to be mindful of here is balance. Too much muscle will slow you down and create a negative effect on your movements. Believe me, this is not something you want to happen when you're out there on the field.

# Rule #3 - Focus on Becoming Lean. Do Not Exercise like a Bodybuilder

Whatever you do, don't become tempted to get too big. This is not a body-beautiful competition. What you're after here is a lean, mean, well-toned body. To achieve this you will use maximal strength exercises. This is the best way to build just enough muscle for extra strength and added protection.

Your goal here is to have just the right amount of muscle to help maintain consistent performance. Remember, too much muscle will slow you down on the field and affect your mobility.

With maximal strength exercises you have to lift heavy weights. The key here is to only lift them for a small number of repetitions. It will be something like 3-6 sets per exercise and from 1-5 reps per set.

You need to also take adequate rests to recover between sets. It's important to only perform a small number of exercises for each training session too. Remember, you are not to exercise like a bodybuilder.

# Rule #4 - Multi–Joint Exercises Are the Way to Go

The final of the four rules is to work on multi-joint type exercises. You don't want to focus on isolation exercises. That type of exercise places an emphasis on a single muscle or muscle group. It's much better that you work on multi–joint exercises.

This way you get to incorporate more muscles in a single exercise and session. These will include exercises like squats, dead lifts, and bench presses. Others are clean and jerk, lunges and shoulder presses. Make a note of these as they are the ones you need to focus on in your training sessions.

# 31. Not Being Aware of the Other Team's Attempts to Waste More Time

Time wasting is something that happens a lot in soccer. It occurs most when one team is leading in the score and there's not long to go before the end of the game. In these situations, the team leading wants to hold on to that lead. So the team players decide to find any way they can to waste time.

# The Ways to Waste Time

One of the methods used can include a verbal fight with you or one of your teammates. The idea is to distract you and attract the ref's attention.

With any luck, the opponent manages to stop play while the ref books one or both of you. If he succeeds, he has managed to waste a few precious moments as the end of the game draws ever closer.

Opponents of the winning side will also fall to the ground and pretend to be injured. They might even pretend you've hit them if things get desperate. Again, any of these tactics can waste a bit more precious time. Wasting time is harder than it sounds though.

By that I mean it is something the referee will be looking out for. Refs have zero tolerance with this kind of behavior. This is why any time-wasting efforts have to look as natural as possible.

The winning side will also waste time when playing fouls. They will waste time retrieving the ball from the outside in throw-ins, and during goal kicks as well. Another way to waste time is whenever a substitution takes place. It's easy to waste time, but it's not so easy to disguise it.

If you feel that the other side is wasting time, and the ref hasn't done anything about it, be sure to bring it to his attention. The reason to do this is because it will make him more vigilant of the other side. Also, the referee can add extra time if he feels a team is wasting time on purpose.

To stop the opposing team from wasting your time, try to avoid kicking the ball out. You must also never stop the play anytime one of your opponents fakes an injury.

This is especially important when you're certain it's a put on. My advice is to keep playing while the opponent is on the ground.

This way, and providing the ref doesn't blow his whistle, you can use his trick to your advantage. If you don't stop, and the ref doesn't blow his whistle, you have one less player to worry about at that moment.

I've already covered why you must never stop play unless you hear the referee's whistle. You can find that in chapter 24, "Not Playing on the Referee's Whistle."

# 32. Not Fighting for Every Ball

To be a great midfielder you must die for every ball. Whether that's a pass or when you try to recover it from the other team, you have to give it your all every time.

This is the only way to maintain a solid, steady performance on a consistent basis. Anyone who tells you different is either lying or having a different agenda.

The best players in the world of soccer are those who treat every play and every ball as if their life depended on it. They do this because they are passionate about their role in the team. They want nothing more than to contribute to their side's success.

Ask yourself who the best midfielders have been in the past 20 years or so. See if you can identify them before moving to the next paragraph. Think in particular about those on the defensive side of the middle.

OK, take a look now and see how you did. With any luck you came up with players like Edgar Davids, Dunga (Carlos Caetano Bledorn Verri), Patrick Vieira and Roy Keane. They were real warriors not just your usual talented players.

Fans used to love it when Man United played against Arsenal. This was not only to see the teams compete, but also to watch the players Keane and Vieira. The fans were always enthusiastic to see how they would deal with each other on the day.

The fact is that their tenacity and high spirit inspired everyone on and off the field. They were, to all intents and purposes, a side attraction.

I don't mean they weren't great team players, because they were. I just mean they were a joy to watch, and because of that they got a lot of attention.

The ability to get the ball is not just a physical skill but a mental calculation. It is one that's based on determination and expectation. If you don't yet have it, don't worry, you can get it. All you have to do is believe and you're half way there.

Not every player is born a fighter but he can develop into one, if he wants to. Any change like this all begins with a shift in attitude and outlook. The day you decide to become a fighter on the field is the day you start to fight.

Remember this: 80 percent of the time the ball goes to the player with the highest spirit. That's the one who believes he will get it, and so he does, most times at least. And why is this so? Because he does whatever it takes to make it happen.

So as a defensive midfielder the question to ask yourself isn't do I have the required skills to succeed? Your question should be how can I be a warrior on the field?

Once you find the right answer(s) to this question, everything else will start to fall into place.

It means you will intuitively know how to handle the game with the right skills and aggression for a given situation.

Coming up next:

In the following chapters we take a look at how to play good soccer in the different weather conditions.

# 33. Not Knowing How to Play in Rainy Days

Every weather condition has a different set of problems when it comes to playing soccer. The more you prepare, the more you get to increase your chances of success on the field.

Experience is important in these situations, obviously. But if you're not experienced then knowing what to expect will help you a lot too. In this chapter we take a look at how to play soccer when it's wet and rainy.

# Playing Offensively

On a wet or rainy day the ball will be a lot heavier. That means the player with the ball has to exert extra power when striking it. This alone makes the game harder, but it also has some advantages too.

When the rain is heavy or the ground is sodden, the best option might be for an attacker to kick the ball hard in the direction of the goalkeeper. In normal conditions it's not usually a good idea to aim at the keeper for obvious reasons.

If there are other, easier options, then always take them. But when it's wet and the one going for the goal needs to act fast, he should never be afraid to aim in the direction of the keeper.

The reason is because it's difficult for any goalie to catch or deflect a wet, heavy ball with any real accuracy. In fact, if conditions are really bad, he will be relying more on potluck than actual skill.

## Be Alert Anytime the Keeper Tries to Catch the Ball

Playing in the rain makes it easier for attacking players standing near the goal area to do follow ups. It's not unusual for the goalie to drop the ball or slip while trying to save it in the rain.

This opens up so many great opportunities for nearby rival strikers. They can, and often do, get to score goals in these situations with follow ups.

Always stay alert any time the keeper leaves his goal to catch a ball. Just know that a goalie, even a good one, will often fail to maintain full control over a ball that is soaking wet.

## Play Lots of Crosses

When it's raining, you can play as many crosses as you like. Do this especially when the rain is heavy as heavy rain makes it hard for the goalkeeper and his defenders to see the ball.

# Playing Defensively

When your play defensively in wet conditions you have one main aim. That is to prevent your opponents from shooting as much as you can.

As you've already seen, shooting in wet weather causes a lot of problems for a goalkeeper. Whatever your position is in the middle, as a midfielder, you will always be your team's first defender in situations like these.

If the opponent going in to score is close to you, secure the keeper whenever he goes out for the ball. In these situations you must expect that your goalie will drop the ball or fail to catch it altogether.

Always remember that he has restrictions in his movements on wet ground. So if he blunders, and there's a chance he will, will, clear the ball away as soon as you can.

No one likes to play soccer when it's raining or when the field is soaking wet. But the reality is that games do still go on in these conditions. For this reason, it's important that you practice and prepare for competing on wet and rainy days.

# 34. Not Knowing How to Play in Windy Days

When the wind blows, the ball moves faster in one direction and slower in another. There's also a chance that the ball will change its direction, either a little or a lot. This all depends on the strength of the wind of course. A sudden change in ball direction is even more likely when there are strong gusts present.

# Playing Offensively

When you play on the offense, try to shoot at the goal more often than usual. The presence of strong winds gives you an opportunity to fire at the goal any time the wind is behind you. It's even better if that ball changes direction as it approaches the goalmouth.

## When the Wind Changes Direction Your Crosses Deceive Defenders

When the wind is with you, send lots of crosses. In these situations your teammates have an increased chance to score from headers. Most defenders hate playing against the wind and it's not surprising. Wind restricts their movements and alters the ball's direction. Windy conditions can destroy a defender's chance of clearing crosses from his penalty area.

# Playing Defensively

When you play on the defense, always apply pressure on the ball holder. Likewise, when you play against the wind try to apply early pressure on the other team's players.

This is especially important for the one holding the ball. Your aim is to block and prevent as many crosses as possible.

If you play on the defensive midfield, you need to acknowledge your defensive teammates. Always be aware of where they are at any given time. Your job here is to collect and sweep up any shots that deflected from them.

## Outnumber the Attackers in the Penalty Area and Don't Wait for the Cross

If the rival team is smart they will send lots of crosses to take advantage of the wind; the way you did during the first half. When this happens, you need to make sure that the number of your defensive teammates in the penalty area is more than the number of rival attackers.

Also make sure you don't wait for the cross to come to you, Instead, you should go to meet it every time. This is to avoid any ball deflection that may occur near to your goalkeeper.

Always be ready for balls that deflect back from the goalkeeper. He won't have the luxury of catching some of the shots if there's a strong wind. This is an even bigger problem for him on days that are gusty.

Strong gusts create all kinds of problems for every player, but the goalie has the hardest time of all. The most frustrating thing for him is the sudden change in ball direction as he attempts to save shots at his goal.

Whatever approach you take to help your performance in various weather conditions is fine. That's as long as it works for you and doesn't break any of soccer's rules, of course.

# 35. Not Meditating Before Games

You might not believe this, but a lot of professional soccer players meditate. In actual fact, they attribute their calmness and high state of focus to meditation. It's true; these big tough guys have daily meditation and mindfulness routines.

Former soccer players, Dennis Bergkamp and Peter Schmeichel, swear by the power of meditation. They claim that they meditated not just once but twice on the nights before their games. They did this especially when they are having a big game the following day.

There are a couple of reasons why you might want to take a look at meditation. One is that other soccer professionals use it, and the other is that meditation has the science to back it up. It has shown to boost self-confidence, self-esteem and general wellbeing.

Meditation also increases optimism and self-awareness. Not only this, but meditation increases ones awareness with both time and place (the "now"). The latter is a skill that any midfielder should and must have in order for him to become great.

Some texts suggest that meditation has been around since 2600 BC. Other accounts say that meditation has been with us for as long as humanity as we know it has existed.

All you need to know is that millions of humans, from all walks of life, have used meditation for a very long time. They can't all be wrong, meaning it must have proven benefits otherwise no one would bother with it.

The real benefits of mediation are too many to list. I would say that it's more useful today than at any other time in history. After all, constant distractions and interruptions surround us all day every day. Stress levels have never been so high, and so a calming of the mind can only be a good thing.

So what can meditation do for you as a soccer midfielder? Well, meditation will enhance your ability to make critical decisions. It will also help you to manage distractions and feel more in control. Both your mood and your breathing will be more controlled too.

Believe it or not, but most of us don't breath the right way; we breathe too quick and too shallow. Most of us never give much conscious thought to the way we breathe; it's just something we do.

But here's the thing: the way you draw breath can affect your physical and mental wellbeing. Needless to say, when this happens you cannot possibly perform at your best.

The majority of us draw breath about 20,000 times a day. Experts would consider this to be too much under normal, non-stressful situations. These are short, shallow breaths that we take. But we would benefit more from longer, deeper breathing. Meditation teaches you how to do this.

## We Used to Breath Properly

When you were a baby, you would breathe naturally. Babies tend to take deep, relaxing breaths from their abdomen. If you watch a baby sleep, you will see its stomach rise and fall rather than its chest. This is not so with adults, not now, not in the twenty-first century. Most of us only ever use the top third of our lungs, and it's our chest that rises and falls, not our stomachs.

I'm not going to go too deep into meditation in this chapter. There are plenty of great books and articles out there that are far more qualified on the subject than I am. But I do want to highlight the basics of this ancient practice. I feel it's important to point out the benefits that it can give to you as a soccer player.

You see, when you get to regulate your breathing on a regular basis, great things begin to happen. To start with, you become calmer and more mindful. When this happens, you get to boost your performance during soccer games, and that can only be a good thing.

If you meditate shortly before a game, something special happens with your muscles; they become fully replenished. What that means is that your muscles get just the right amounts of energy-giving oxygen they need. This is something which is invaluable for any sportsperson.

At the end of this chapter, I will give your some basic guidelines for meditating. If you do decide to have a go (recommended), then you should have no trouble finding other, more detailed articles and resources. There is plenty of free stuff on the web that can help guide you toward developing your own meditation routines.

Before we move on to the mediation guidelines, let's first take a look at the more specific ways that mediation can help you with your game.

## Meditation Can Help You to Keep Your Eyes on the Ball

Monitoring the "ball" and keeping the "ball" away from danger, is a midfielder's key responsibility. You may wonder why I highlighted the word "ball" twice. I did this to mark how important this point is.

Too many CMs and DMs lose focus and lose sight of the ball at wrong times during a game. The consequence of this is that it costs their teams a lot. They lose out on what could have been easily intercepted balls. What often happens is that the midfielder focuses on the wrong things.

He will fix his stare on the opponents and their feet movements. What he should do is focus on the ball, and only the ball. At the end of the day it's the ball, not the opponent or his feet that he needs to get hold of. Anything other than the ball is of low priority.

## The Fly Swatting Analogy

Have you ever tried to kill a fly with a fly swatter? If yes, then you will know just how difficult this can be. In fact, if you don't keep your eyes fixed on the fly, swatting it becomes an impossible task.

Well, the same thing happens when you're attempting to intercept a soccer ball during a game. In this case the ball is the fly and you are trying to get it. Unless you keep your eyes fixed on it, meaning only the ball, your task is much less likely to succeed.

There are two ways to enhance your focus so that you can keep your eyes fixed firmly on the ball at all times. To be any good at defending, you need to develop sticky eyes. Those two methods are Air Hockey and meditation.

# Air Hockey

Try to dedicate a suitable amount of your time to play air hockey. You can use a real table or play it as a video game, it doesn't matter which. Air hockey is one of the best mental games for midfielders, or any other player, who needs to improve their focus. Here's why:

Air hockey improves your response times. And it helps to maintain those sticky eyes I was referring to as well. Best of all is that air hockey is a lot of fun too, which makes the training sessions enjoyable.

Get a friend to compete with you, or if that's not doable play the video game version. If you opt for the video game, be sure to set it on an advanced mode as soon as you are able. I can guarantee you will develop sticky eyes using this method. That's providing you put in the time to practice of course.

# Meditation

We've already looked at the benefits of meditation. If it all sounds a bit too "spiritual" for you, and not your thing, then try to view it in a different way. Look at meditation as nothing more than sitting still in a quiet space for a set period of time.

After all, that's what it is, in its most basic form at least. Set aside just 15-30 minutes a day for a week, and at the same time each day. You will know by the end of your seven day trial whether you want to carry on or not.

OK, as promised here is a quick guide on how to meditate. If you want to go deeper into this, just take a look online. The internet is awash with some great sites dedicated to the practice.

## How to Meditate

- Wear something loose-fitting and comfortable.
- Find a calm space to practice.
- Switch off your mobile and any other distracting devices.
- Get into a comfortable sitting position with your feet resting flat on the floor.
- Close your eyes and focus on your breath, breathing in through your nose and out through the mouth.
- Feel your stomach rise and fall as your breath. Your chest must remain still.
- Do not get up or fidget for the duration of the meditation.

## Know what to Expect

You will have all kinds of thoughts and distractions when you first start to meditate. This is quite normal, so don't think you're failing if you find it hard to still the mind at first. Let any thoughts come and go from your mind.

Don't try to control them or get into internal conversations. Just allow them to happen. Your aim here is to just watch your thoughts as an outside observer.

OK, so the above guide is the most basic level of meditation. As I have said earlier, if you feel you want to get deeper into this, there is a plethora of great advice and information on the web.

# 36. Not Having Enough Motivation

Motivation is an internal process. It is the thing that makes someone progress toward a certain goal. Some players are naturally motivated. What that means is they don't have to be motivated because it's their normal state. Others are not so lucky, especially when the going gets tough.

This latter type needs motivating, or to put it another way, they need a push to get them moving. If you're in love with the game and your soccer position, it will be much easier to motivate yourself than if you're not so passionate. To succeed in any area in life, not just soccer, you need passion, ambition, patience and lots of hard work.

For every one great player you know or know of, there are 1000s of others who failed to make the grade. These are the majority of hopefuls that get lost and forgotten.

Every player who has made it into your memory had that special something. But make no mistake about it, none of these guys got to where they are with ease. Not even those who possess natural talent. Talent without work is a useless attribute.

Players with no natural talent can still make the big time. They have to apply extra of everything to get there, but some do, despite the odds.

They make it because they are passionate about playing soccer. Their determination is unwavering. They never give up, not even if others tell them they have no chance of making it.

## Supply Outstrips Demand

The demand for talented players is a lot less than the supply. There will be tens of thousands of young players the world over who all aspire to reach the big time.

However, there will only ever be a tiny handful of available slots in professional soccer to accommodate the few. So the competition is tough, to put it mildly.

Only the best of the best will stand a chance. The players who do make it are not necessarily more talented than those who don't. They just managed to stand out in some way, that's all. This is what got them noticed. Anyone who's looking for that lucky break has to do the same.

## What the Talent Scouts Look For

Talent scouts look for passion and potential. They can spot things in players that others can't see, even the players themselves.

People are often surprised at how a lesser talented player is sometimes chosen over a more talented one. It's because the scout saw something in that player that set him apart.

Never underestimate potential. Some good defenders might have reached their potential. Others might still have plenty of growth left in them. Talent scouts are good at spotting these things.

## Prepare Yourself for the Good, the Bad, and the Ugly

There are no free rides in soccer. To make it into the big time you have to be willing to go beyond pain, disappointment and failure. You have to keep pushing forward no matter who or what stands in your way.

This is the only approach that will see you reach the results you want. And the only way to keep moving forward through thick and thin is to develop that special type of motivation. For this you need a real strong reason(s), something that will push you past failed attempts and setbacks.

## Knowing Your Reason(s)

It doesn't matter what your reason is for wanting to be a great midfielder as long as it's a strong one. It might be that you want to prove to yourself and to others you have what it takes.

Maybe it's the money and the glamour of the game which motivates you. Although to be honest, if it's money over soccer, your chances of making the big leagues are slim at best.

Your reason might be nothing more than your immense love for the game and the dream of turning your passion into a career. You know what they say about that:

*"If you love what you do, you'll never have to work a day in your life"*

It's true too. Very few people actually get to turn the things that they love into a living. Most folks work in jobs that they don't particularly like but have to do nonetheless. Everyone needs an income to survive, of course.

And because of this, we often take whatever job pays the best, whether we like it or not. Anyone who loves what they do for a job is truly blessed.

Dig inside yourself and dig deep. Once you find out what this strong reason is, hang on to it and keep reminding yourself of that reason(s). This will become the engine that drives you forward.

# What It Takes to Be a Star Player

You will need a great amount of motivation. Your energy, effort and mental toughness should be relentless. You must go through injuries, exercises and strict physical conditioning programs. You have to strive to be better than everyone else.

Doing all this won't come easy. You need to be willing to go beyond pain, disappointment and failure. You will encounter setbacks along the way, that's inevitable.

But you cannot let setbacks dampen your spirit or affect your motivation. Nobody can put your off, and if they try, you work even harder to prove your worth.

If you don't feel all that motivated right now, don't worry. It's quite normal after reading something like this to think that it's all just too much. But if your heart in really set on becoming a star player, then one or two good night's sleep should have you feeling re-energized and ready for action.

# A Final Word

My final word on this is that you mustn't look at hard work as some kind of lesson in torture. Just because something is tough, that does not mean it can't be enjoyable. Actually, the opposite is true in many cases. Enjoy the journey and relish the challenge.

With the right attitude and outlook, you will excel to whatever level it is you're aiming to do well in. Will you become professional?

There are no guarantees for that, but the more you get noticed the better your chances. What I do know, however, is that inaction, or dreaming about stuff, never achieved anything.

# 37. Not Having Good Leadership Skills

Anyone who displays leadership shows signs of motivation. If you want to become a world class midfielder, it's important that you can lead.

A good leader can motivate his players no matter what happens on the field. The best leaders can inspire others. They can do this even when they themselves don't feel motivated at the time, for whatever reason.

# Three Great Defensive Leaders

Let's take three great defensive leaders to illustrate the importance of leadership. The former French midfielder, Patrick Vieira is one. The former defensive-midfielder, Didier Deschamps, is another.

And the former Spanish central defender, Carles Puyol, is the third. All three of these guys demonstrated consistent motivation. They could inspire their teammates no matter was going on around them.

Vieira was the captain of Cannes at the age of just 19 years old. Deschamps managed to keep his teammates inspired through tough competitions. He succeeded to lead players like Zidane, Henry and Robert Pires, to win their first world cup title. He did all this despite the many problems the French team had before the beginning of the tournament.

I watched Deschamps play in the 1998 championship. You could see how juiced up his teammates got once they saw him intercept a ball or make a great header. He was impressive to say the least, and that was despite his age and despite being short at just 1.74m.

He would motivate any teammate who messed up with a wrong pass or a wrong shot. He would do this by letting him know that it's okay, and that the team still needs him.

The key here is to maintain momentum. If that's lost, so are motivation and a winning attitude. Deschamps is a pro at keeping momentum high.

To become the great midfielder that you want to be, you too must show real leadership skills. Your job is to transfer confidence, faith and determination to all your teammates. This is even more important when the going gets tough and you guys are behind in the score.

Nobody likes being around a weak midfielder, someone who is quick to admit defeat. Anyone who gives up at the first sign of danger will never be a real asset to any team.

You'll find that all the best midfielders, especially Registas and DMs, display strong character. They have something within them that prevents them from surrendering.

It keeps them going when the going gets tough. They will push and motivate their team toward victory right up until that final whistle. These guys couldn't throw the towel in even if they wanted to.

It's not in their makeup. They have that winning mentality that I often refer to, and no one can take it away from them.

Of course there will be bad days, or even a bad run or a poor season. Other times the team's performance will be so poor that you want to throttle the guys rather than encourage them. But you don't do it. You're better than that. You understand that soccer is a team sport.

That means sticking together through thick and thin, the good times and the not so good. You understand the importance of the wider team effort. For you, your ego, your name, your reputation and your own enjoyment is not as important at a win for the team.

If the team's strategy is not working, you look for ways to fix it. When players are feeling down, you pick them up. You are a midfielder, and that means you protect your guys and keep the ball safe. You do this come rain, come shine, come hell or high water. You lead by example because you are a winner, and winners never quit.

In life (not just soccer) most people look for someone to take the lead and guide them. Most of us aren't natural leaders, but we can learn to become great leaders if we aspire to be.

A good leader helps to motivate those who are unable to motivate themselves. This is especially important when the chips are down.

Midfielders that have these qualities are not only rare but also valuable as players. If you want to make a living out of soccer, as a midfielder, you know what you have to do, you know now what you have to become.

# Tell Your Teammates How Good They Are and You'll Inspire Motivation

Arsenal's manager, Arsene Wenger, has a great quote about this topic. He says:

*"A football team is like a beautiful woman. When you do not tell her, she forgets she is beautiful. It's the same with a team. When you don't tell them they're good, they can also forget."*

And this is exactly what you should do.

Take the leader's role and praise your teammates after every good move they make. I too am a firm believer with giving credit where credit is due.

A pat on the back doesn't take much but it can mean a lot to the one receiving it. Let the players know their worth. Make them feel superior on the field and they will play in a superior way.

Inspire your team and create as much positive energy within the squad as you can. Don't give them a hard time after every mistake, they will be feeling bad enough about it as it is. Giving someone grief on the field won't pick them up and make them play better.

But it will dampen their spirits and make them play worse. We all make mistakes, and we should learn from them (positive) and not get blamed for them (negative). A good leader does not have to go into a rage to get things done. Those who do are out of control, and that's no way to lead or gain respect.

Always remember, good leadership is all about the people. It is not about the plans and it's not about the strategies. It is all about motivating people to get their job done.

A well-oiled team knows the plans and they are familiar with the game strategies. You don't have to lead by organizing these things. Look after the players and the players will look after their roles.

# 38. Not able to Save the Game When Needed

Any type of strong performance you make on the field will have a positive effect on those players next to you. Likewise, if your performance is poor, and consistently poor, that can have a negative effect on those players next to you. How does this happen? I will explain.

Anytime you make an outstanding performance, and succeed, it lifts moral instantly. It might be that you scored a goal, assisted, or kept your penalty area safe.

Whatever you did, it will motivate and inspire courage in your teammates, especially the defensive ones. In other words, the better you play, the better your teammates will play too. It's what we call the knock on effect.

## The Slippery Slope Down

Imagine that you and your team are playing blinding soccer and you're all on top form. Now imagine that the team you're up against is playing even better than your side. At the start of the competition you are all highly motived because it's still early in the game.

But what if the other team retains their upper hand and continues to dominate. And despite your best efforts, you can't seem to break through their defense lines. It won't be too long before enthusiasm begins to dwindle and moral drops.

Now imagine how the other side must be feeling in the same game. They will be feeling great about themselves. They will also notice your drop in motivation and take advantage of that.

They will be on a high, a real winning streak, and their adrenaline will be pumping. So they play even harder in their attempts to completely destroy your moral. Figuratively speaking, they are preparing to kick a man when he's down.

It is times like these that a good team leader sees what's materializing early on and comes to the rescue. If he's smart, he does this before his side completely loses their edge. He rallies the team together, despite things being fluid.

He then gets all the guys to recompose themselves. With any luck, he manages to get everyone back into the game with renewed vigor. It's now time to make a comeback.

Comebacks are never easy, but neither is giving up. And the further down a team gets, the harder it is to make a comeback, but it is possible, and it does happen.

Your ability to make a comeback centers in the mind, not in the body. You know how to play well as an individual and as a team. You've already done that earlier on in the game. Times like these need a little AA, or Attitude Adjustment.

# Making a Comeback, Taking the Lead

I have seen true leadership many times over the years. One such example was when midfielder Steven Gerard, MBE played at Liverpool. In this game, Liverpool was playing against AC Milan in the 2005 UEFA Champions league final.

They called this game the Miracle of Istanbul. It was one of the best comebacks in the history of the Champions league.

Steven Gerard managed to lead his team to victory against the Italian giants after being behind in the score at 0-3 by half time. In the second half, Liverpool launched an impressive comeback.

This was all thanks to the leadership of Gerard. They managed to score three goals in just six minutes, leveling the scores at 3–3.

During this game, Gerard scored a solo goal for his team in the 54th minute. He then immediately went to get the ball from the net, pushed his teammates forward, and helped them lead the game to a penalty shootout. In the shootout, Liverpool beat AC Milan 3-2 on penalties.

In fact, during the same tournament, Liverpool was about to get eliminated from the knockout stages. Again, Steven Gerard showed exceptional team leadership skills and scored a game winner in the 95th minute. This was only a few seconds before the game ended.

This is how a leader should affect his players. He instils confidence in them, whatever the situation happens to be. He lets them know that nothing is over until the ref blows that final whistle.

He motivates them to press on with hope and determination, to do whatever it takes for them to triumph. Being down in the score, and so close to the end of the game, should not be any reason to admit defeat.

# Manage Your Players Through Hard Times and Hostile Atmospheres

You should always be able to deal with hostile fans. This is never a nice experience but it's something that happens in soccer nonetheless.

Usually, hostile chants will come from the rival team's fans, but not always. There may be times when your own fans become hostile toward you or another player on your side.

This usually happens when they have a "reason" to hate you. This reason will usually be for some major blunder you made which cost your team dearly in an important tournament.

Many players lose focus when playing in abnormal situations. It's certainly an abnormal situation when angry fans express their disgruntlement toward a player.

Another is when opponents frequently attack you whenever the referee is not looking. This is a tactic that opponents like to use when you're far behind in the score as it has more effect then.

As a team maestro, captain and role model, you are the one who should keep team spirits high. You set an example by leading by example. You remind your players what they represent to the side and the fans. You show them how to block out any negative distractions and focus on only that which is important.

If you can control and push yourself, no matter what comes your way, your teammates will most likely follow. Remember, both negative and positive behavior can have a knock on effect. It makes sense therefore, to choose the latter over the former.

In soccer, full backs and wingers who play on the sides will receive the most verbal abuse. So will anyone playing corners and throw-ins. You must have heard the saying, "take the bait." Well, when fans taunt you, this is exactly what they are trying to get you to do.

They hope you will take their bait and respond in a negative way. If you give those fans your attention, or if you allow them to upset you in any way, then they have won. You will lose your focus on the ball, and probably your momentum for the rest of the game.

No one, except the other team, wins when you lose your cool. As soon as opponents see you lose your edge and your motivation, they will take advantage of your weakness.

Never forget; how we think affects how we feel, and how we feel affects the way we function. It's all connected. So thinking negative thoughts makes you feel bad, and that in turn affects the way you perform on the field.

Even motivational team leaders are human. That means there will be some days where you are more vulnerable to external distractions than others. For some players, taunts and negative jibes roll over them like water off a duck's back, but not everyone is the same.

The secret to dealing with external distractions which affect your mood, is to learn how to best channel that anger or frustration.

In other words, use it to your advantage. Let me explain. The idea is to keep everything as simple as possible. You do this by following this rule:

Whoever or whatever bothers you creates a negative energy within you. You need to use that energy as a force to push forward. Put simply, channel that energy into your game. Don't let it sit inside your head and fester.

And don't express any anger or frustration toward those who are trying to upset you. As a leader, you cannot afford to let such things affect you in a negative way, not in front of your team. You're a role model, and you can, and must rise above all these kinds of things.

# 39. Not Being Able to Quickly Recover After Making a Serious Mistake in the Game

For some players, it only takes one bad mistake and they lose their focus for the rest of the game. Some will even ask for a substitute to take their place. This is especially the case if their error leads to the rival side scoring a goal.

Everyone has good days and bad days, and that includes soccer players too. When any player has a bad day, for whatever reason, it can be hard to hold his nerve and remain confident.

Because of this, he is prone to making more mistakes and errors of judgment on the field. These are errors and bad plays that most likely would not happen when he's feeling good and confident.

There are times when a mistake he makes will be so big that it looks as though his team might lose because of it. In such situations it's hard to stop thinking about the incident.

One big blunder can affect the entire team too, not just the player who's floundering. This is especially true if his bad mood and worsening play is obvious to those around him.

And if he makes more than one slip up, he can't help but feel like an unwanted presence on the field. The more his side is behind in the score, the more difficult it becomes for him to continue on.

Some of you reading here will be able to relate to all these things. Situations like this are not that uncommon. But they don't have to be as bigger deal or as intense as many make them out to be.

Most can relate to the above setbacks as young amateurs trying to progress in the game. But it is only those who use their mistakes to learn and develop from who get to shine above all others.

The only way to avoid the spiraling down of moods and emotions is to change the way you think. Words like hard, difficult and impossible are the words of average people.

They are what optimists refer to as excuse words. These are words used to justify incompetence or poor performance. That might sound a little harsh, but isn't it true?

Because you've read down this far into the book, I guess you have come to realize something important. I think you must know by now that this book is NOT for average midfielders or day dreamers. This book is for those who aim high and think big.

Or at least the readers of this book will want to know how to aim higher and think bigger. It is a book for go-getters, not fantasists who never move past the "if only" stage.

Those of you reading here will want to leave your mark. You will want to make an impression in both soccer and midfielder history at whatever level you play at.

So my advice to you is to leave the "excuse words" for the average players to excuse themselves with. For you, look at hard, difficult and impossible situations as challenges. Don't look at them as something to fear or run from.

## Live in the Moment

There is a lot of power in the "Now". Living in the moment is not something most people get to master. Our minds tend to wander between the past and the future, skipping over the present moment as if it has no use.

All I can say about this is that you must form the habit of staying in the now, especially when you're playing soccer. The power of NOW is incredible once you get to embrace it.

This is something that can benefit you in ways you wouldn't imagine. When you think about it, there is never ever any other time. It's always NOW, and it always will be NOW.

Yet so many amateur players are anywhere but now in their thoughts. All too often they run "if-only this," or "what-if that," scenarios around in their heads.

Learning from the past and preparing for what lies ahead are things that have their place in soccer. I'm not disputing that. But the past and the future have no place when your focus needs to be firmly in the here and now.

To maintain your peak performance after making a huge mistake you need to be present. That means you have to be in the NOW and deal with events as they are, at that precise moment in time. To dwell on what's just happened is a recipe for failure.

If your team is not performing well, and you're far behind in the score, the only way out is to perform better. It means the team's performance has to change right NOW. Understand that you can't bring about any changes if your focus is anywhere but in the present moment.

The way to do this is to isolate your mind and not think about the past. You must also isolate your mind so that don't visualize a miserable future outcome. I know that a shift in mindset is easier to say than it is to do.

Even so, nobody ever said soccer was an easy game. In fact, if soccer was easy, then serious players wouldn't enjoy it. They would most likely opt to play something else instead.

Staying in the NOW, when you most need to be in the present moment is a skill that you can develop. Let us look at how to get that shift in attitude, which is so crucial to the role of midfielder. I will do this by first explaining something outside of soccer, so just bear with me here.

Albert Einstein once said:

*"You can't solve a problem with the same mentality that created the problem in the first place".*

That quote explains a powerful yet simple logic. Even so, we don't always live by it as I will explain in a moment. You might just want to read Einstein's quote over a few times to get the real gist of it. Also, look at your own game and see if there is any connection to Einstein's quote in the way you approach things.

OK, here is a non-soccer example to illustrate a typical approach made by many of us. It is something that looks stupid when written down, yet it is still the kind of thing so many of us do nonetheless.

Let us suppose that a Trojan virus has infected your computer. Because of this infection your computer no longer works as it should do. In situations like these, the first and most logical thing for you to do is to run a full system virus scan.

You might also run an anti-malware program too, and anything else you might have to attack the problem. You are desperate to get rid of the intrusion so you waste no more time and get right onto it. This is a logical response to this particular problem.

Now, let's say that your virus checker could not find any suspicious files. You know the virus is there. Heck, you're getting lots of intrusive popup messages every few seconds telling you as much.

Worse still is that your virus scan seems to have created even more issues by removing critical files that your system needs to function properly. In this case, your problem has just gotten a lot worse by your attempts to fix it.

Someone with a negative mindset might try to solve the problem by repeating what they have just done. So they continue to run and rerun a full system scan. They do this even though the results are always the same, or worse, after each new attempt.

They are wasting their time and their energy. Their patience is also wearing thin with each failed attempt. They become agitated and experience enormous stress. All that's happening here is that the person is getting nowhere real fast.

Yet despite it all, they continue to rinse and repeat the same failed procedure. Some might even say it's a form of madness to continue in this way. I would agree that such an approach does seem crazy. Yet haven't we all been guilty of this behavior at some time?

Einstein also said:

*"The definition of insanity is doing the same thing over and over and expecting different results."*

The difference between a successful personality and an unsuccessful personality is not hard to define. It is simply the thoughts we feed into the mind that shapes our thinking. False beliefs and negative thinking are what bug a pessimistic mindset. If you can relate, don't despair. This doesn't mean you're doomed to a life of misery and failure on the field. That's providing you are open to positive change.

To change the way you view things, you have to move things around a bit. By "things" I mean thoughts or 'old stinking thinking' as I like to call it. To get rid of old negative thinking patterns you have to replace them.

You cannot simply try to ignore them and hope they will go away and never bother you again. The only way to get rid of old thinking is to replace it with new thoughts. These will be more positive thoughts and beliefs.

One way to transform your thinking is to find a good mentor. This can be someone who is dead or alive. It needs to be a person who thinks and believes in a way that you would like to think and believe. Once you find someone who succeeds in a way that you would also like to flourish, you then need to tell yourself this:

*From now on, this is exactly how I will think and act to achieve my own goals.*

What you are doing here is borrowing the mindset of someone else. You're only doing this to kick-start your thought process.

This is just until you get to develop your own change in thinking. Don't worry, you are not trying to become a clone of another person, in fact you couldn't do that even if you tried.

All you are doing is applying their thought patterns and approach to life and planting them into your own psyche. From here, these new, borrowed thought patterns will shape over time to work with your own unique personality and approach.

If you are ready to ditch your old mindset completely, just know that you can do it. Understand that it hasn't helped you to succeed so far, which is why you need to change.

Duplicating another person's mindset is a proven technique. It is an approach that has succeeded for many players who adopted it as they developed their game.

*What if I don't want a mentor, what then?*

You don't have to have a mentor if you would sooner not. I think the mentor approach is the best one, but you can still do this alone if you prefer. All you have to do is just recognize your own negative thinking patterns. Once you know what they are, you can then get to work at swapping the negative with the positive.

There is only one way to maintain mental toughness and stay emotionally strong when the game is not going too well. And that is you need to be able to pick yourself up and recover pronto so that you can move on with enthusiasm and determination.

The way to change your outlook all starts with a shift in how you think. If you haven't found the mindset of a mentor to borrow, you can start to develop your own from scratch.

Here are two simple rules that you need to be mindful of before you proceed. These rules will lay the foundation for you:

1. Understand that blaming yourself and thinking about the past always hurts you, it can never help you. So STOP blaming yourself

2. Remind yourself that successful defenders forget past happenings on the field. They are always in the present, thinking about what to do NOW so that they can succeed with their next move.

You can develop your mindset just like you can develop skills and muscles. In fact, there is very little that you can't improve with regards to your physical and mental wellbeing.

All you need is a strong desire to change and follow that up with positive actions. When you do this, change becomes inevitable.

# The Power of Audio

It's a good idea to set a couple of hours aside in the day to listen to audio books. Look for titles that talk about succeeding in life and successful people in general.

You can include the 10 X Rule in this if you like, in fact I recommend it. I used to listen to the 10X Rule in audio book format early in the morning, before I began my day.

I would then listen to some more chapters again in the evening, usually just before bedtime. When you sandwich your days like this, with positive learning, it helps to build a whole new mentality. This not only helps you on the field, but in everyday life too.

When you start to think and act the way successful people think and act, you will become more successful in your own endeavors.

Work at these things and you will become amazed at just how quick you get to recover on the field from bad situations. Of course there will still be those times when you or your team makes major mistakes, or falls behind in the score.

But the way you react, or not, as the case may be, will be so much different. Strive to be successful and you will succeed.

It's actually quite a simple formula when you think about it. Not always easy to implement and develop, I know. But at least the basic principles are uncomplicated.

# 40. You Are Afraid of Getting Hurt or Injured

In some situations players, and especially backs and defensive midfielders, fear going after the ball. Other times they are afraid to perform a certain move or a certain type of tackle. Can you guess why? The reason is fear. It derives from the notion that they might get hurt real bad or suffer an injury.

No one wants to get hurt or injured, of course. Pain aside, accidents on the field can take a player out of action, and for a long time too if the injury is a bad one.

There are, however, two types of fear. One is justified (healthy) fear, and the other unjustified (unhealthy) fear. It's important to be able to distinguish between the two.

A player's reluctance to play as well as he could do, all because of fear, is usually unnecessary. At least in most cases it is.

It's not much use to a team to have a player on side who only half commits. Having talent and physical capability to be great midfielder is not enough on its own. He will never be of much use if he refuses to use his skills in certain situations.

There is no room for cherry picking what you do and what you don't do in soccer. This is a position that requires courage to go into situations that are difficult.

Such a situation might mean a full-on physical challenge with someone bigger and tougher. Yet these things cannot and should not deter any player from doing his job.

What these guys need is a strong boost of determination and courage. Some will develop it whereas others will never break through this psychological barrier. It doesn't take much to guess who will go on to succeed and who will remain as just another Average Joe midfielder.

Knowledge is all power, and it's a lack of knowledge that creates fear within these guys. It is only when a midfielder can put fear into perspective that he gets to move on.

It is not weak to have fear. It is a normal human response to things that threaten us. Not even big tough guys relish the thought of getting hurt or injured. It makes perfect sense to protect ourselves from these things. This is what we call healthy fear.

All living creatures, and that includes humans, are hardwired to avoid pain and suffering. Without healthy fear we simply could not survive and thrive as a species. But as I mentioned earlier, there's healthy fear and there's unhealthy fear. In other words, fear has its place but it needs to be healthy and kept in perspective.

As for the role of midfielder, any unhealthy fear brings with it caution, and with caution comes hesitancy. Any midfielder who hesitates will underperform; it's as simple as that.

Most fears in soccer are unfounded, meaning they're not justified. This is why it's so important to put fear into perspective. This way you get to understand the difference between justified and unjustified fears.

Once you put fear into perspective, your mindset will change for the better, along with the way you play. Your goal here is to have less fear and more bravery in all areas of your game.

When you remove unjustified fear from your mind, you become more courageous on the field. That means you will take more action, and that will improve the outcome of your game.

And the braver you are, the more confident you become in your ability to fulfil your role as a midfielder. A great midfielder is tough, not only physically but mentally too.

If you already play as a midfielder then you are already brave to some extent. The question you need to ask yourself is am I brave enough, could I be any braver? Developing bravery is more to do with psychology than physical ability.

If you're a midfielder who is hoping to play at the professional level, then you must not allow fear to dominate your thoughts. Instead, limit fear to a specific set of situations, that is, those which warrant healthy fear or caution.

Far too many people these days have evolved into namby-pambies. By that, I mean they are afraid of just about everything, including their own shadows.

They have become so fearful that it prevents them from living life to the full. To succeed as a midfielder means you have to play a tough game. There is no place for over-caution or unjustifiable fears in this role.

Some players start off fearless and then go on to become more fearful over time. They develop a particular fear for a certain type of play. It might be because they suffered hurt or injury at some point. Or maybe they know of, or saw a situation that triggered fear inside their minds.

## Mikel - Injury Prone - Arteta

Let's take a look at Mikel Arteta. He plays as a defensive midfielder for Arsenal. Arteta has suffered a lot of injuries since he joined the club in 2011. With each new injury he lost a bit more of his fire.

Over time, he started to become less aggressive when playing in the middle. This resulted in him losing too many easy balls.

He became too cautious because he got too fearful. He worried about getting hurt or sustaining yet another injury. When things like this happen to a player their value becomes less.

In Arteta's case, his lack of aggressive play saw him lose his position as the team's number one stopper. The job went to his teammate, Francis Coquelin. Worth noting here is that his French counterpart is 10 years younger than he is.

Some center backs become afraid of a hit to the head or breaking their nose. You can see this in the way that a lot of amateurs play. They develop the habit of closing their eyes when going in hard. You can often see them half-heartedly reach for a header lest they get injured.

Once again, what happens here is that the players have either lost their nerve or have a twisted perspective on fear. To get rid of this fear you have to put things into the right perspective.

This is not difficult to do at all. It just means you have to look at the facts. Ask yourself how many serious injuries there are in the majority of games.

When you do this you get to realize that the probability of suffering hurt or serious injury is actually quite low. Because of that you have to then ask yourself if it's worth losing the ball or conceding a goal, all because there's a slight chance you could get hurt. There is even less chance of a serious injury. It's important to remind yourself of these things.

# Why You Feel Afraid

Your fears center in your mind. You feel afraid because you think too much. That's it, in a nutshell.

Let me explain in a little more detail. Fear on the soccer field is not real or justified, at least not in the majority of situations. It is a byproduct of the thoughts you create inside your head. Danger is real, but fear is a choice. It's important to distinguish between the two things.

For you to play well means you have to have the courage to get stuck in. You need relentless determination and tenacity. And the best way to kill all these things off is by thinking too much about what might happen. Stinking thinking can only result in self-doubt. Any doubts you have about your ability to succeed in a situation will result in failure more often than not.

When you think too much about the wrong things, and not enough about the right actions, there will always be negative consequences. It will destroy both the quality and quantity of your actions. This applies not only to soccer but in all areas of life.

# How to Deal with Over-Thinking

Try to stop thinking about anything other than your next actions on the soccer field. In short, stop thinking and start doing, just let your instincts take over. If you've been playing for a while, you should intuitively know how to deal with most of the common plays.

As you know, soccer is about timing and fast actions. Over-thinking and fear are two peas of the same pod. Both of these things will see a dramatic delay in your timing, and you know what the consequence of that can be.

When you look at fear for what it actually is, you get to change your perception of it. Try to see F.E.A.R as False Evidence Appearing Real. After all, this is exactly what it is in most situations on the field.

Again, the best way to proceed in these situations is to think less and do more. Keep moving and take action right away. Make a deal with yourself by refusing to let fear mess with your game.

Many midfielders play for years without sustaining a single injury. You might think that they are just lucky. It's possible, luck might have something to do with it, but it won't be the only thing, that's if luck plays any part at all.

My guess is that these midfielders avoid injury because they're fast acting and confident. Those who are slow to act and overcautious bring a lot of problems on themselves. Being hesitant just invites problems that otherwise wouldn't exist.

Hesitancy makes players more prone, not less prone, to accidents and injuries. It's a bit like the slow and overly cautious drivers on the roads. They think they are safer, yet they are more prone to having an accident, or causing one, than other drivers. The drivers who move forward with confidence and make quick decisions are the safest of all.

I think it's quite apt to end this chapter with a couple of quotes. It will pay you to remember these:

*"We die if we worry and we die if we don't. So why worry?"*

The above quote is so true. Of course we are going to die whether we worry about things or not. Some things are worrisome, but a lot of what we worry about is so unnecessary. Worrying about suffering a rare injury will definitely hinder your progress.

Wrapping yourself up in cotton wool takes the fun out of your game. And without the "fun" element, there's just no point. Be mindful of the fact that thinking will never overcome fear, but action will. This brings me on to the final quote:

*"The only thing we have to fear is fear itself." ~ Franklin D. Roosevelt*

# 41. Not Learning from the Pros

Learning comes in two parts. One is study, and the other is action. The learning process is defunct without both parts. One of the best ways to learn how to do something, the right way, is to take lessons from the pros. The way you do this is to watch videos of these guys, and watch them a lot.

The great thing about moving pictures is that you can play them over and over. Another wonderful thing about film is having the ability to freeze-frame, fast forward, rewind and play back in slow motion.

The ability to learn something well is a skill. The willingness to learn is a choice, and one that all great midfielders choose to do.

It's important to understand that you are always striving for progress, never perfection. Perfection is an unrealistic goal. If you ever did reach perfection, which you won't, there would be nowhere else to go and nothing else to do.

Each time you strive to learn something new you will always discover something fresh. There is no graduation here, but there is potential to reach great heights. At least there is for those who embrace learning and never stop.

You are reading this book because you want to enhance your physical and mental skills. You can learn a lot from reading these pages, but reading on its own is never enough.

This is why I always suggest including other medium into you learning process. This includes things like TV, video, and watching live games. These should all be a part of your overall learning routine.

Remember what I said earlier about the difference between watching and studying. So don't just watch soccer's greatest midfielders play, STUDY them. Try to mimic their style. Look for things that you might not have otherwise thought about doing. Learn how to discover the more latent flaws in your own style from the mistakes that you make. Embrace failures and setbacks as great learning tools.

To take your game to the next level you need to have a healthy obsession for your position and ambition. It is only when you do this that you can speed up your learning process.

Be ready to always take action and never stop learning. Set yourself constant challenges. At the end of every day set a new challenge.

Vow to know something, or know how to do something new. This will be something you didn't know about, or know how to do, the day before. It could be something quite big or quite small.

The size of the new discovery is not the point. The point is to just learn. Learning is a mode that you can get into. The more you learn about the things you love, the more you want to know.

Here's a word of caution. If you fail to get into the learning mode, you will not only fail to progress but will actually regress. Not learning something new on a regular basis is a trap.

It is a trap that all too often results in procrastination. It doesn't mean you don't want to learn new things, it just means you can't be bothered at that moment in time.

It's a trap you want to avoid at all costs. The only way to avoid this trap is by learning some fact, or some new skill, every day, big or small. Learning is a healthy habit and one that I urge you to form.

As you know, playing professional soccer is not a long term career. That means you don't have too much time to waste, not if you're to flourish at an early age. You might be young now, but the retirement age for most professional soccer players is also young.

This is why you need to develop that winning mindset, and the sooner you can do that the better. Showing potential at a young age is the only way to stand out so that the important people get to notice you.

Professional soccer is not a career that you might want to look into when you're in your mid-twenties. Before you reach the age of 18 or 20, most of your soccer skills and attributes should be well-developed. I would say to about 60-70% percent of their full potential. Of course there is always room for improvement at any age and at level in soccer.

But you won't be able to start from the bottom up if you're already in your 20s. The passion doesn't have to die out though, just because a player is older. But if you want to reach the professional level, and play for the big teams, then soccer is a young man's pursuit.

## Remember the Power of NOW

Earlier in the book we looked at the power of NOW. This also applies to the learning process. Just be mindful of the fact that excuses have no place in your pursuit of greatness, so make sure you don't go looking for them.

The only method you need to embrace is the get-up-and-go approach. This is what will help you to stand out from the pack, that's providing you are consistent with it.

When you're into the action side of learning, also remember the power of repetition. Repeat the same play over and over until you get good at it.

Once you get to check a new skill off as "learned," switch over to the next one that needs mastering. Don't delay because you are now in full leaning mode. It means your mind is tuned-in to the learning process.

When you are like this you are at your very best. You are in a position where you get to learn faster and with better results. Don't break your momentum now that you have it. This is the approach and mindset of high achievers.

OK, let's now look into another proven method that will help to boost your development. Here we look at video again, only this time it is video of you, not of other, professional players.

## Videotape Yourself to See How You Really Play Soccer

Using cameras as a learning tool can prove invaluable to your progress. Having such footage like this can reveal a lot about the way you play. Video can highlight things to you about your game that you might not have otherwise noticed.

## Video Exposes All That Is Hidden

Video can help you to identify your strengths and detect any weaknesses you might have. These are things that are not always easy to spot when you're actively playing soccer.

Even when your coach is monitoring you, he will not always get to see those smaller, more latent things about your playing style. This is where video becomes invaluable.

Even tiny errors in your game can have a big impact in the way you play and the outcome of a given situation. It is only when you get to identify flaws in your game that you can get to work at fixing them. This is why you should embrace the power of video footage.

Thinking about stuff after an event, and also having things explained by others, is also useful. Even so, the more tools you have at your disposal the better you will fare. It is only when you see yourself in pictures (moving and still) that you get to appreciate the power of the lens.

Your primary aim with video is to find out all there is to know about yourself and the way you perform on the field. It is the only way that you get to see your playing style for what it really is. My suggestion to you is to use cameras, and use them a lot. Once you get into the habit of doing this you won't regret it, of that I am certain.

# The Ease of Videoing Yourself

Thanks to modern technology you now have a real advantage over the players of yesteryear. I would say that most of you reading here have Smartphones, Tablets or Phablets at your disposal. All these devices have inbuilt digital video functions as standard. This means you can get a friend or teammate to film you practically free of charge.

What you must never forget is the fact that however good you are, or think you are, there is always room for yet more improvement. No player should ever concede to the notion that he's about as good as he's likely to get. This just isn't true. There is always room for more.

If you were to give me video footage of any amateur player, I could tell you all sorts of things about the individual. These would be things that he most likely never knew about himself. It really wouldn't take me long to spot the good and not so good areas of his playing style either.

More than 95 percent of the time I am right in my assessments. This is not because I have some kind of magic skill for spotting these things. It is simply because I have learned how to observe a player's performance as opposed to watching it.

What you need to take from this is that there's huge power in the lens. Understand that things can show up on recorded footage that is not always obvious by other methods of observation. From video you get to identify bad footwork, distractions, any lapse in reading the game, and so on. It all comes out on film, once you know what to look for.

Obviously you cannot film yourself and play soccer at the same time. You will therefore want to get someone who is willing do this for you. It's better if that person has a good knowledge of soccer as they will now what to record and from which angles.

It's also better if they know how to use a camera to best effect. I also suggest using a tripod whenever possible.

## If at First You Don't Succeed…

The first few attempts to record you in action might be a bit hit-and-miss. Don't worry if this is the case.

Unless the one doing the recording is a professional, you should expect to adjust things as you go along. Just keep at it and you will soon have some fabulous footage taken from the best shooting angles.

Note that video recording is not a replacement for help and advice from your coach and other players. It is simply a valuable addition to this. You will always get some great advice and tips from your coach and other more experienced players.

But there is nothing quite as valuable as seeing yourself on video. If you want to fix, fine-tune, and add new skills to your toolkit, then start to record your performances without further delay.

# Discuss Your Footage with the Coach

When you get the first decent video footage of yourself, make sure you share it with someone qualified. It needs to be someone who will look at it objectively with you.

My advice is to start by discussing your findings with your coach. Whatever you do, don't end the discussion without setting a fixed plan. Between the two of you, decide what the next course of action should be.

You need to come up with a plan that helps you to overcome your weaknesses and/or gets rid of any mistakes you have identified.

# All Players Benefit from Video

The French goalkeeping coach, Christophe Lollichon, joined Chelsea in 2007. During his time at the English club, Lollichon has coached some great goalies. Petr Cech`s and Thaibut Courtois are two of the most famous. In an interview for Chelsea TV, Lollichon talked about what it's been like to work with two of the world's best goalkeepers.

Christophe Lollichon is a well-known, well-respected coach. Petr Cech said something this summer (2015) that no one expected to hear. He said that he won't sign up for Arsenal unless the club brings along his favorite coach. This shows you how much respect this world renowned goalkeeper has for his coach.

Cech knows that he would never have got to where he is today without the guidance of Lollichon. So what is it that makes Lollichon so special? Well, maybe it's what he said in the interview that explains it the best.

Lollichon said that he and his staff use at least two cameras when they coach. They do this to track every single move that any of the keepers make on the field. Lollichon also said that he spends from 2-3 hours going over the most recent footage with all his goalies. They look at what he has done wrong and what he has done right.

In other words, he doesn't just tell him to fix this or improve on that. He sits down and takes quality time with his keepers, reviewing the footage in great detail.

Only when everyone is on the same page and understands it all, do they then work on a plan. They look at how best to fix any flaws and improve any existing strengths before the next game.

## Compare Your Mistakes

When you view video footage of yourself there is no place for overprotective behavior. That means you have to look at your mistakes objectively and not get upset if your coach or anyone else finds fault in something you did, or did not do.

You might also want to compare your video footage to famous midfielder players. Use YouTube and other video sharing websites to find clips of them. Cover your problems from all angles. Ask yourself what the professionals might have done, or did do, in the same or similar situations.

Compare all your plays with other midfielders. Also look at your take-offs and the decisions you made at the time. Look at your foot work as well. Look at how you position yourself in general. In short, you need to cover everything about your game. Leave no stone unturned as you scrutinize the video.

I hope that I have got the value of video footage over in this chapter. It really is an invaluable tool. If it wasn't, all the greats would not bother to use it, both field players and goalkeepers. To record yourself, and then watch yourself play, is the best and most effective tool you have.

There is nothing that comes as close as video with regards to learning about your mistakes on the field. It's also the fastest method you have at your disposal, at least once you have some good footage it is. This is because you get to see things that might have otherwise gone unnoticed, or unnoticed for a long time.

Many younger and older midfielders alike will often repeat the same mistakes over and over. These are sometime quite subtle and hard to spot under usual conditions.

This is why video is so invaluable. Don't forget too, you should have the option to play footage back in slow motion. You will definitely be able to pause, stop, rewind, and replay. These are obviously not things you can do in real-world situations.

Today, video is cheap, it's effective, and it's portable, so make sure you use it. You'll be glad you did.

# 42. Not Knowing How Your Teammates Play

Study your teammates the same way you study your opponents, if not more. There are a number of things you need to pay particular attention to. In this chapter we go through each of these in turn.

## Study your Teammates Favorite Foot

One of the most important skills any playmaker or CM should possess is the ability to send good passes.

However, his passes will never be much good unless the teammate getting the pass receives it well. That means he must receive the ball at ease and from the best possible angle.

The best player to pass the ball to is not always the one who's least pressured by an opponent. It's not even the one who's running into an empty space. Quite often, the best player to pass the ball to is the one who's in a position to receive the ball with his dominant foot.

The reason for this is because that particular player can then move the game on right away. It means he's good to go, without wasting any time adjusting his position and switching or changing his balance before making his next move.

To make these quick, better informed decisions, you need to be mindful of two things. One is that you must listen to what you teammate asks you to do.

The other is to be familiar with their style of play. This means you will know where and how they like to receive their passes before you send them the ball.

# Know How and When They Run

You must be familiar with the positions of all your teammates. You need to intuitively know where a teammate is going to run to. You also need to know where he will be place himself next before he even makes his move.

Some attackers love to move closer to the middle. They do this so that they can start the attack by themselves.

Others prefer to play outs-and-ins or the opposite, by moving wide on the flanks and then going in deeper.

However they play, you should be familiar with all these small details of your teammates. Once you are, you get to perfect your game and better your chances of succeeding as a midfielder.

# Know the Attacking Tendencies of Each Player

Some skilled dribblers will only need you to create space for them. You do this by moving with the ball or running solo, taking a defender with you. The defender then gets to penetrate deeper and move closer to the opponent's goal. Other players, especially CMs, will advance a little as they wait for the ball. Once they get it, they fire well-aimed shots at the opponent's goal.

These guys can give you excellent options when you're playing wide and not quite sure what to do with the ball. By knowing that you're playing next to guys like Steven Gerard or Paul Scholes is comforting.

You know who is waiting for opportunities and where they're positioned. This allows you to stop, change direction, and assist the free CM in the empty space toward a nice goal.

# 43. Not Knowing How to Score from Fouls

Not knowing how to score from fouls is not an uncommon problem for midfielders. In this chapter we take a look at the problems and solutions surrounding this.

**Case 1**: Direct free kicks that are close to the penalty area.

Scoring from this type of free kick has more to do with your shooting accuracy than your shooting power. Most of the time, just getting the ball to reach the goal ensures you will score. This is regardless of the ball's speed or its power.

In these situations, you need to be careful when striking the ball, and avoid putting too much power into the kick.

Watch how Lionel Messi scores from his free kicks. Messi is one of the best three players to score from close-range direct free kicks in the world.

During the last UEFA Super Cup against Sevilla, which Barcelona won by 4-3, Messi scored from two direct free kicks. He played these close to the edge of the penalty area.

The third of his free kicks was barely saved by the keeper. The ball then directed towards Messi's teammate, Pedro Rodriguez. From there, Rodriguez then scored the winning goal for Barcelona.

When you study Messi's free kicks from that game, you will get to see how he plays them. To start with, Messi stands close to the ball rather than far away from it. Before he starts to shoot he walks, not runs, to get just one or two steps closer to the ball. He then kicks the ball with controlled, intermediate power. Most impressive is his accuracy as the ball heads toward the goal.

If you listen to the commentary during his first goal you will hear this phrase:

*"It has no power but he (Messi) glides it into the corner."*

He did the same against Real Madrid, and again against Atletico Madrid. And he did it again in the Super cup. So he's not just lucky, Messi knows exactly what he's doing. He has a winning technique that is incredibly effective.

# Think about the Ball's Direction

Avoid playing free kicks in the same direction as the goalkeeper. That's unless you have a strong foot and have developed a technique that will blast the ball past any keeper who tries to stop it.

Most of us don't, I'm afraid, but there are a handful of players that do.

These include Roberto Carlos, Mario Balotelli and Zlatan Ibrahimovich. We're talking about balls that can reach 120+ Km/Hr here. Such kicks are rare and have the power needed to perform free kicks that most goalies stand no chance of saving.

But like I say, the majority of us don't have such power. That means you're better off opting for the classic way that players like Messi use.

**Case 2**: Direct free kicks that are far from the penalty area.

In these cases you must combine shooting power with accuracy. It is the only way to get that ball into the net.

Unlike the first case, you will have to keep a little distance from the goal. This is so that you can create enough movement and power to launch your kick. In these situations, the ball needs to maintain its power as it travels across a greater distance.

# Juninho Pernambucano - The Free Kick Master

Andrea Pirlo learned how to shoot free kicks by watching videos of another Brazilian player called Juninho. Juninho, in case you haven't heard of him, is by far the best free kick taker of the last 25 years.

Search anywhere on the internet for best free kick takers in the 20th century. You will always find the name Juninho Pernambucano at the top of those lists.

Pernambucano spent eight years with Olympique Lyonnais. He helped the team dominate French soccer by winning seven consecutive French leagues. In total, he scored 75 goals for the team. Forty four of those goals were from free kicks.

Juninho had the ability to score from anywhere on the field and against any team and any keeper. He had goals from near the penalty area and far from the penalty area.

His goals also came from near the corner, close to the center line. He scored against great keepers Iker Casillas, Oliver Kahn and more besides. He was a true master who you could learn a lot from.

So how did Pernambucano play his fouls? Well, it's perhaps best if the man himself explains it. Here's how Andrea Pirlo quoted his success in his autobiography:

*All you need is the right swing and voila…You have a goal. My own Eureka moment arrived when I was sat on the toilet. Hardly romantic, but there you go.*

*The search for Juninho's secret had become an obsession for me, to the extent that it occupied my every waking thought. It was at the point of maximum exertion that the dam burst, in every sense of the term.*

*The magic formula was all about how the ball was struck, not where: only three of Juninho's toes came into contact with the leather, not his whole foot as you might expect. The ball needs to be struck from underneath using your first three toes.*

*You have to keep your foot as straight as possible and then relax it in one fell swoop. That way, the ball doesn't spin in the air, but does drop rapidly toward the goal.*

*That's when it starts to rotate.*

The moral of this account is that we can all learn from others, even the greats from the greats.

# 44. You Force the Pass

When another player calls for the ball he might not always be your best option to pass it to. Despite this, you feel compelled to pass the ball to him regardless, and so you do. In many situations like these the ball can get lost, intercepted or taken from the receiving player soon after he receives the ball.

The lesson to learn from this is not to let others pressure you into making your decisions for you. If you have 3-4 players around, make sure you make the bests decision.

What you mustn't do is just give in to whoever is calling the loudest. You need to be confident and strong enough to do what you think is right, and not what another player tells you to do.

The midfielders who have the highest percentage of missed passes are the ones who:

- Tend to force their passes too much.
- Surrender to any teammate pressuring them for the next pass.
- Panic when surrounded by 2, 3 or 4 opponents, and make hasty decisions because of that. When panic sets in like this, the result can be a poorly thought out pass.

You might have noticed a connection between the three common mistakes above. That is, they are all things which center in the midfielder's mind. We have "forced," "surrender," and "panic." None of these things has anything to do with the midfielder's physical abilities or inabilities.

The most successful midfielders are the ones who can maintain the upper hand on the field. They don't just pass the ball to the first teammate who calls for it. They have their own vision and they trust their own judgment and their own skills.

Remember what I wrote about Arjen Robben, and how he sometimes appears selfish on the field. There's no question of doubt that he is selfish in many ways. But at least he always plays the game his way, once he has the ball in his possession.

Quite often he succeeds and sometimes he will fail. Either way, he always takes responsibility for his own actions. I have seen him score many wonderful goals with his style of play. He performs some fantastic runs and feints too.

The last thing Robben's does is pass the ball to the nearest teammate, not if he can help it. He would never give in to a pushy player either, that's for sure.

A lot of people disapprove with his selfish style, and that's understandable. But at least he triumphs from his approach more often than not. He is, at least, his own man and never lets other players force his decisions.

To be excellent at passing, especially if you are a playmaker, you need three things:

1. Be prepared to pass in unexpected places. Or at least take the unexpected option, even if it means running with the ball yourself. Before making a pass, check where the majority of opponents are located and pass the ball somewhere else. This is the correct and most logical option for you to choose most of the time.

2. Trust your skills and be confident in your decisions. This is better than surrendering to anyone asking for the ball, not really knowing what their next plan of action might be.

3. See the full picture. In other words, before you receive the ball, check over your shoulder and see if there are any available spaces around you. Once you find somewhere, make use of it and pass the ball toward anyone running into that space.

When you stay ever mindful of these three things you will go on to develop your own independent style. Of course it's important to be a team player, but that doesn't always mean jumping to the demands of the nearest teammate calling for the ball.

Sometimes it will be the right thing to do and other times it won't. Once you get to know the difference, and act on your own decisions, then you will go on to excel as a great midfielder player.

# Final Thoughts

In Forty-four Midfielder Mistakes to Avoid, I have shown you everything you need to know about how to become a great midfielder. We have looked in detail at how soccer's greats have managed to build a reputation for themselves.

My final piece of advice to you is quite simple. In fact, it is so simple and short that I can sum it up in a single phrase:

## Take Action!

Despite the simplicity of this message, it is still the main stumbling block for many players.

I'm serious. There is a lot of lost talent out there all because the players never followed through with their dreams.

They didn't just lose out because they were at the wrong place at the wrong time either. It's because they failed to take action.

Whenever someone doesn't follow through on their commitments, they can't expect much to come of their dreams. Can you related to any of the above? If you can, then you need to come up with a better plan. Failure to act will result in the situation remaining the same. To sum that up with a quote:

*"If you always do what you've always done, then you'll always get what you've always got."*

Your hopes and dreams of becoming a great midfielder will always stay as just hopes and dreams if you fail to act.

Yes, it's sometimes hard to take action. And yes, it can also be inconvenient at times; messing with other plans you might have.

It can be demanding too, painful even. But nothing is quite as disappointing as looking back on your life when you're older and having regrets. You can see it all the time, as older guys ask themselves that age old question:

*"I wonder what would have happened if only I had…."*

You get to fill in the blanks.

Please acknowledge this very important fact. Every single LW, RW, CM, DM or AM you know the name of, even the most mediocre of them, has taken a great amount of action to achieve his goals.

So here's the deal with this book. Promise yourself that you will take positive, regular action based on what you now know. Aim to do this at least 10 times more than everybody else you know.

Stick with the plan no matter what. Create check lists if that helps. A bit of box-ticking can be a great motivational approach as you work through your action plan.

Get others involved, surround yourself by people who support and encourage you. Likewise, distance yourself from those who try to tell you that you're not good enough.

I hope that this book has inspired you. We have covered a lot and used many real-world examples to illustrate certain points. We've looked at what to do and what not to do. We have looked at the many tools and techniques that you can use to your benefit.

These are the things that soccer's greats have used to help them excel in their careers. Yet despite all this, none of it is of any use unless you now put your newfound knowledge into practice.

So again, my last word to you is to take positive action and follow your dreams. Don't give up just because someone tells you you're not good enough. In fact, that is even more reason to press on than ever. Keep believing until you realize your dreams. Embed this quote into the forefront of your mind:

*"The only real failure in life is the failure to try."*

Remember to always, always, always believe in yourself. Do this even when stuff doesn't seem to be going according to plan. Actually, do this especially when things don't seem to be going according to plan.

I hope that you have enjoyed reading this book as much as I have enjoyed writing it. By now you should be inspired and ready to take your game up to whole new levels.

Never forget that progress is not possible without some degree of failure and setback along the way. In actual fact, failures and setbacks are instrumental in the learning progress.

It's important, therefore, that you view failures in a constructive light. That means, see them as something which helps, not hinders, your overall progress. Be mindful of this whenever things start to get tough.

You must believe in yourself. If you don't, then those who you need for encouragement and support won't be able to believe in you either.

Let us end with a quote from one of the legends of English soccer.

*"Some people tell me that we professional players are soccer slaves. Well, if this is slavery, give me a life sentence"* ~ *Sir Robert "Bobby" Charlton.*

(1937: former English footballer; still the all-time highest goal scorer for England and Manchester United).

End.

I sincerely wish you all the best in all your endeavors to succeed.

Mirsad Hasic

# About The Author

Mirsad writes all of his books in a unique style, constantly drawing connections between his past experiences and his reader's goals.

This unique approach means that you can avoid undergoing the same injuries, frustrations, and setbacks that he himself has endured over the years.

He can't produce the results for you, but what he can do is promise that you WILL reach your goals - guaranteed – providing you follow his tips and advice exactly as he outlines them in his books.

1. 1-2 passes that confuse defenders. They get me most of the time!
2. Catenaccion italiano.
3. Juininho free-kicks.
   Pirlo free-kicks.
   David Beckham.
   Hakan Calhanoglu.
   pabrick vieira.
   steven Gerard.
   # Arturu Vidal penalties.
   Leighton Baines Penalties.

   Matt le Tiss penalti
   Roy Keane.
   Giggs.
   Inzaghi.
   Bergkamp

4. watch the team the Galacticos.
5. Iniesta passes.
   Baine's penalties and freekicks.
6. Try Focusing and blocking outsi distractions.
7. Theo walcott, Arjen Robben. Ball-hugg
8. Dr. Evan Joseph soccer.

Made in the USA
Lexington, KY
17 November 2018